TAKE YOUR POSITION
Daughter

Redefining Pain by Turning It Into Purpose

Monica Ibarra

Take Your Position Daughter

Copyright © 2016, 2021 by Monica Ibarra

Published by T.N.T. Publishing

ISBN-13: 9780692715819

All scripture quotations are from the NIV®, NASB®, NKJV®, NLT®, AMP®, and WEB®. All Rights Reserved.

*Please note, the name satan/lucifer and other words/titles/names associated with him are intentionally not capitalized, even if it is grammatically incorrect.

*"The enemy" is also used to refer to satan.

Printed in the United States of America

Table of Contents

—Dedication—

This book is dedicated first to my husband, Fernando Ibarra, who has never wavered in his commitment to loving me. Thank you for gently loving me when I couldn't love myself and for supporting me when few did. Your persistence to support and love me gave me strength to stand and not give up. It is because of you and the sacrifices you have made that this book is possible.

Secondly, this book is dedicated to all the women who I hold in my heart that I have yet not seen. These are women who have cried themselves to sleep many nights. Those that people pass by because their greatness is not detected and they wrestle with feeling insignificant. These are women who search to have their deepest needs met. For those who want more, this book was written for you. For the purpose of you seeing hope, truth, and finding the Love of Father God, and never, ever returning to a life without passion and purpose.

—Introduction—

Hello, I am looking forward to sharing my life with you. I have prayed for you before you ever received this book. For over twenty years, I have worked with women of all ages and ethnicities as a skin care consultant. For years, before going into the ministry, I had the opportunity of getting to know many women and understanding that for the most part, every woman struggles with some of the same issues.

During my time of working in the beauty industry, I realized most women will try just about anything to feel better about themselves. Every woman wants to know and feel she is loved. Every woman wants to feel and look beautiful and will begin to wither if they don't.

Women can become very creative in masking the pain they carry, and some masks can be worn for so long that they no longer realize they are wearing one. But, eventually, the masks become heavy and uncomfortable. They help temporarily while in the presence of others, but no amount of masks can take away the pain that is deep down within her soul. In order to heal, we must go to the root of what is causing the pain. Otherwise, nothing purchased, no beauty treatments, or aids of any kind will last long enough or reach deep enough to bring the healing in which she so desperately needs.

I know this story far too well. My personal life story is filled with chasing things and people, only to realize that eventually, one runs out of things to chase. Even after giving my heart to the Lord, my life as a Christian was one lived in chaos in my household and my marriage. For years, I lived in an emotional raging storm and depended on prescriptions and other "crutches" to get me through life. As a result, both my marriage and my children suffered. Even though I didn't know it, my emotional outbursts were actually reactions directly related to the deep wounds of my past.

Although I was a Christian, I felt tormented and trapped. I knew I needed healing, but I didn't know how to find it. I needed value and love but couldn't depend on others to give it to me. I could recite scriptures, but I didn't know how to apply them to my life. I didn't understand how to be free from these vicious cycles.

For years as a skin care specialist, I heard the sad stories of many women. Stories they probably didn't even share with those closest to them. Do you know what I learned? I learned that many of us have been abused, physically or emotionally. Many of us have been rejected as children, had a father who could not love us tenderly, or endured a severe tragedy. Many of us keep looking for love from people who cannot give it and are walking around like dead people, without passion or zeal and just enough life to get through the day. Most of us just endure and try to get "over it." Behaving like it never happened, or by just trying to get through it as quickly as possible. So, we don't even want to talk about it. Some families and cultures are especially good at sweeping things under the rug. As little girls, we are told, "Just get over it" or "Don't talk about it."

Carrying shame is daunting for a person. While working in the beauty industry, I learned that women who had larger bank accounts could afford more options to make them feel better. Plastic surgery clinics are filled with women who believe if they could just change something on the outside, they would feel better on the inside. Women with less money, will do the same. They will hide money from their husbands, take out loans, or even get advances on their next paycheck, just so they can feel better about how they look. But, here's the thing, those things are only temporary fixes; because the problem they carry is not cosmetic. Instead the problems are rooted deep inside of them. I was one of these women.

Cosmetics aren't the only thing women use to mask their pain. Some have eating disorders. Some women are held bondage to the gym, (not saying working out is not good), and some women feel they can't be alone and need a partner at all times. Others have to go shopping, while some rely on anti-depressants, alcohol or other stimulants, and perhaps other people to make them feel better. Within all of these women is a voice that is waiting to be released.

It is time to arise! Time to come out of hiding and to become whole. It is time to be heard. No amount of highlights or cosmetic surgery will make your soul well. Believe me. I know! Eventually, we can no longer run. Eventually, we come face to face with the pain, even if we do not understand where it is coming from. Sooner or later, we recognize we hurt deeply. Inside, there's an emptiness, a pain, a rage, shame, anger, frustration, a place we don't talk about because we are so busy looking like we've got it under control. All the while, our soul is crying out, "Pay attention to me! I need help. Listen to me!"

If you listen to your soul, and bring it to be healed by God, the only One who can heal a soul, you will find the storms within will be calmed, and you can have peace at all times. Don't you want that? I know God wants it for you, and I believe if you keep reading and allow the Holy Spirit to work in you, you will walk forward and upward, leaving behind some weights that have been weighing you down.

At the end of some chapters in this book, you will find an exercise for you to complete with the help of Holy Spirit. You will also find at the end of some chapters a place to write notes, the thoughts you have, what you feel God speaking to you about, and a prayer. Keep this as a reference in your walk with God. Please say the prayer out loud so that your heart can hear it because faith comes by hearing. As you say these prayers out loud, I believe the Spirit of God will reveal Himself to you.

Also, there is a workbook available through Amazon, ("Take Your Position Daughter Workbook"), which can help you recognize destructive patterns. I suggest after you read each chapter in this book, go to the workbook and complete each exercise, one chapter at a time.

How much you engage by using the tools available in this book and the workbook will determine how much you receive. My prayer is that you would be fully committed and engaged in your healing process and know God is fully committed and engaged to you. May you sense the Lord's embrace as you set time aside and invite Him as you go through this book.

—Chapter 1—

What Does God See When He Looks at Your Soul?

It is imperative to understand that the first step of healing is to make sure you have given your life to Jesus Christ. Since Jesus defeated the grave, life is in His hands. If we want more "life" in our lives, then we need to submit our lives to the One who gave His for ours.

Without Him, we cannot heal. With Him, we receive a Father's love and the power and comfort of the Holy Spirit. If you have not already received His family, I invite you to. You will never make a better decision because when you accept His love, you will accept His power to transform your life to have meaning and purpose like never before! If you have already accepted His family and you need more of His light in your life to walk more whole and more healed, I am so glad to have you join me in this endeavor. Thank you, for embarking on this journey of transformation with me, leaving one state of being and advancing into another.

There are many facets to transforming into the things of God. After all, we are triune beings that need to encounter the love and mercy of God with our spirit, soul, and body. Many people do not realize they are being held bondage to soul ties. Soul ties are ties within the soul that can prevent you from moving forward in life. Soul ties are ties that have kept you bound by to situations, people, or circumstances. Any situation that has happened in the course of your life that has left a negative imprint on your ability to truly walk in purpose can be a soul tie.

Before we submitted our lives to God and His ways (either because we chose not to or we simply did not know we needed to) we couldn't grasp the consequences of not living under His protection and His standards. Sexual activities can make way for highly destructive soul ties. Once the DNA of another person comes into your body, their cell structure has become part of you. Just like STD's transfer from person to person, soul ties can transfer from person to person, too. It is very important that soul ties are broken and the end of chapters of those relationships are broken correctly, otherwise the residue will follow. This goes for sexual assault as well. I have personally had to break both kinds of ties off my soul, so that my soul would no longer respond from that place of familiarity. I will cover breaking soul ties later (I will discuss how to break soul ties in Chapter 8).

Rejection from people or addictions to people or objects also need to be dealt with in the soul realm. In order for you to break any habit, you must deal with the soul first. For your soul is your true self, your mind, will, and emotions. The condition of the soul is revealed by what is coming through your mind, will, and emotions.

In this book, I will use my life as an illustration of what God does with everyday people who say "yes" to being transformed into His likeness. It is my sincere desire to reveal to you how God reversed the patterns of thoughts that handicapped my ability to hear Him clearly and prevented peace in my life and home.

I was stuck between two worlds, my past and my present. I so wanted to respond the way the Bible instructed me to, but I was stuck on an emotional roller coaster driven by my emotions. I could not function as the Christian I so wanted to be like until I allowed the Great Physician to heal my soul and embraced seeing God in a way I never imagined.

Throughout this book, I will share six keys that God taught me to stay healed, after He healed my soul. By staying on the path paved through the six keys, you will be led to your full purpose and destiny. You will learn how to set boundaries, know how to enter the secret place where nothing can hurt you, and receive revelation of His love for you. I will also share some of my most personal stories and supernatural encounters with God.

As a little girl growing up, I had so many hopes and dreams. However, as I began to reflect in my early thirties, I realized I had not walked in any of them. My marriage seemed hopeless and not at all like the marriage I had envisioned. Not only was I a mess, but I was highly discontent. Discontentment can leak right through and bring even more pain than one began with. I would rise in the morning just to make it to bed at night. Although I was so glad to be a mother, I missed out on so many blessings with my children by trying to compete and keep up with other moms who had seemingly perfect lives. It seemed I had no purpose except to clean the house, take care of the children, provide meals, and continue to juggle working outside of the home.

When I worked full time, as I went off to work in the mornings, I saw women walking their dogs with their babies, and I would wish I could stay home instead of taking my babies to childcare. However, years later when I did stay home, I heard my friends talking about their careers, I found myself thinking how nice it would be to have bathroom breaks and lunch with adults. It seemed I was always discontent. I've learned dissatisfaction comes from an inward battle. I was so dissatisfied with me. No matter how many times I went to Bible study, or Sunday services, I had not embraced me. I attended these events to grow in knowledge and theory, but I did not attend them to make peace with myself and God. Eventually, God revealed to me, that the little girl inside of me had not healed. So no matter what was in front of me, whether much or little, I would never come to a place of freedom, contentment, and self-embrace until I freed her.

But what did that look like? When my husband and I went to counseling before we had children, I read a book on the inner child within. I really didn't pay much attention to it, because it seemed a little far-fetched at the time. Now it makes sense to me. As one who had labeled herself a follower of Christ, I came to a place of wanting so much to have joy, peace, and contentment, and my transformation began with one simple but vulnerable question to God, *"What do you see when you look at my soul?"*

I came to realize, by the leading of the Holy Spirit, that my soul was infected, and therefore it contaminated my thoughts, which corrupted my present life. Would I, could I, be so bold as to allow God to heal me and reveal all truths to me? And could I trust Him to care enough about me to do it?

I knew that for God to heal me, I had to take the time to get to know Him well enough to trust Him. I began to study what the Word of God said about who I was. It all seemed quite beautiful and hopeful, but with the infection within my soul, the truths were not getting through. I had to allow the Word to give me a bath. To remove the "dirt" my past had left behind and the image of myself that was branded on my soul. This led me on a quest of self-discovery, a discovery of knowing God deeper, and a journey that led me to embrace myself as the daughter of the KING. In order to embrace myself and take ownership of the Word for myself, God needed to expose the tactics of the enemy. He needed me to know that I needed Him and I could not receive full freedom without Him. This led me to my first step towards freedom. I needed Him.

There were many red flags that revealed my soul was sick. After living a destructive lifestyle, my soul was crying out for help. Souls cry out for help in many different ways: sickness, depression, oppression of many kinds, insomnia, rage, division in the home, anger, addictions, pride, fear, shame, eating disorders, night terrors, anxiety, personality disorders, and mental disorders, just to mention a few. Because of a childhood filled with abuse, childhood rape, destructive relationship patterns, dependence on others, rejection, father issues, trust issues, infidelity in marriage, controlling tendencies, tormenting fear, and oppression with many types of packaging, I could not walk in confidence, because I had too many layers that weighed me down.

My soul needed to be touched by the living God, and I knew that once He healed my soul, the healing would flow into every part of my life. You are just the same. God healed me and transformed my life. He can and will do the same for you!

Some of us were born and raised in homes without affection, tenderness, and unconditional love, but I can assure you, the voids left by those needs not being met are opportunities for the LORD Himself to fill. Wherever you lack, there is an opportunity to seek the Lord to fill it with His greatness. The great news is that the more you have been disappointed by the lack of love, acceptance, and nourishment, the more excited you become when you realize God can become all that you have not received from people. I assure you, I have walked in those shoes. God has a way of using what the enemy has brought for harm and turning it around into a story of victory.

Today, I am so grateful people deserted me (although I wasn't at the time) because to the degree God is needed in a person's life, is the degree to which God can fill them. Imagine a glass of water that only needs a specific measure to be filled to overflowing. If it can only contain so much liquid, one can only pour so much in. The reservoir that has less liquid in the glass can be filled that much more. I like to think of grace, mercy, and the love of God just like that. The more you need, the more He is prepared to fill. We can't overcome something that we do not see as destructive. So, how much do you need?

While I was in Bible school, I came to a place of surrender. I really wanted to know God more intimately. I found it was very difficult to trust Him fully because people I had trusted in the past had brought me so much pain. I did not know why it seemed so much easier for others to put their trust in God. I allowed God to reveal to me His truths, and I took a good hard look at myself. I realized I still had so much inside of me that needed to be touched by God. There were so many places within me that were shattered that I did not know where to start. It is a good thing God is the One responsible to complete what He begins! It was then, during Bible school, that I came to a place of wanting to know God for myself and how He wanted to reveal Himself to me, and not for what others said He was. If you want change in your life, you must surrender to the Lord Jesus Christ. As you do, He will fulfill His promises.

"For I am confident of this very thing, that He who began a good work in you will perfect it until the day of Christ Jesus."
~ Philippians 1:6 NASB

Remember to say the prayer out loud so that you can hear what you are praying.

Father, help me to see what I need most right now. Help me see the condition of my soul is greatly linked to the level I have allowed You to come in. Jesus, be my Lord, as well as my Savior. I recognize my soul needs You. I have failed and people have failed me. Wash it all by Your blood and make me new. Reveal to me you are my Healer and my most trusted Friend. Help me give to You all that I have held on to. Help me trust You to do it and believe You love me. Help me see with Your eyes and Your understanding. Help me see my true condition, as You see it. Give me courage as I submit my will, my emotions and my thoughts to you. In Jesus name, Amen.

Your thoughts/what God revealed to you.

_____

_____

_____

_____

_____

_____

_____

_____

_____

_____

_____

_____

—Chapter 2—

Daddy God-The Perfect Good Father

Who are the Daughters of the KING?

"Yet to all who received him, to those who believed in his name, he gave the right to become children of God." ~ John 1:12 NIV

I truly believe many in the Body of Christ do not have a true revelation of their identity as children of God. If they did, they would not settle for anything less than God's best, nor would they allow thoughts of inferiority to germinate in their hearts.

In this chapter, you will have the opportunity to let go of painful memories and disappointments and release them onto the altar of God so that each one of you can receive your Almighty God as Daddy. The One who is the Perfect Good Father! You cannot receive unless you let go of what has disappointed you and brought you pain. You cannot impart something you've never encountered. Therefore, you will encounter GRACE.

To give grace reveals you have received grace. You will see those that have hurt you through the eyes of the cross and through the eyes of resurrection. The cross signifies grace and mercy, and resurrection signifies LIFE. My hope is that you will choose to see those that have hurt you through grace and mercy so that you can receive resurrection power, and understand that because they had not encountered grace and mercy themselves, those who have hurt you could not give it.

The Father's focus was on what the cross would bring. It was His desire to send Jesus because of His great love for you and me. In other words, the Father says we were worth the penalty of torture that Jesus endured. Just like the pain God brings us out of, God wants to use those testimonies to draw others out of their pain. We can't share God's healing, had we not known pain. We can't share His peace, had we never experienced chaos. When God saw crucifixion, He saw resurrection. And not just in Jesus Christ, but He saw the resurrection you would walk in. God sees resurrection in our lives when we invite Him in. God will use the circumstances you have walked through to teach you how to never allow the familiarity of the pain to keep you in a destructive cycle.

Until you let go and renew your mind with the Word of God, you will not heal. Many people are addicted to counselors. Although there is a place for counseling, without the true revelation of the Word of God by the power of the Holy Spirit unmasking roots and destroying them, there can never be full and complete healing. Since we are triune beings, in order to receive full healing, we must deal with the spirit, soul, and body, allowing God's Word to perform "surgery."

Many times we do not truly want transformation because true transformation involves taking personal responsibility, especially in relationship issues. You may be thinking, "If only the other person would change, situations would be easier." However, God searches for people who are willing to be changed by Him so that He can change circumstances. Are you ready for your circumstances to thrive? Me too! Let's go!

Growing up, I lived in a household that only spoke words that brushed the top surface. There was no true emotional intimacy. I found it extremely difficult to trust God as a Father because of my relationship with my earthly father. Abba means "Father", also used as the term of tender endearment by a beloved child in an affectionate dependent relationship with their father. Abba is the same as "Pappa" or "Daddy."

I was never comfortable calling my natural father "Daddy." I so wanted to, but because I felt like he did not know me, nor did I truly know him, I could not call him daddy because it felt awkward. To me, the term "daddy" exemplified tenderness and intimacy. I heard other children call their dads "daddy", and it made me feel as if I were loved less and rejected because I did not have a "daddy-daughter" relationship with my father. We lived under the same roof, yet we did not know each other. He provided food and shelter, but never emotional love, tenderness, or security. If your relationship with your father on earth is one that is or was unfulfilling, it is important to realize that a person cannot give unconditional love if they don't have it to give, especially if they never had it themselves. The truth is, my father was hurting and didn't know how to express it. The only way someone can truly love is by allowing Jesus Christ to be their Lord, for God is Love.

"He who does not love, does not know God, for God is Love."
~ 1 John 4:8 NKJV

No person is perfect. It is much easier to see the wrong in someone else's life before we recognize the wrong in ourselves. Remember who you were before God called your name and you responded. Remember that He has begun a work in you and the process is continual. You must understand that individuals give to the level they have received. Therefore, people can never give what they don't have.

Perhaps your story is similar to mine, perhaps not. One thing is certain, only God is perfect. Since I have progressed in my journey with the Creator, now His name to me is Daddy God. No other name seems closer to how I feel. I realize that unless an earthly father has received the love and adoptive encounter that only Father God can give, he can never rise up in the position as a true Daddy. Unless a man knows God as Daddy, he can't rise up to be a husband who is tender, protective, and nurturing. A woman who has not received God as Daddy, will not be able to rise fully.

When you know God as Father, you live by a standard. When you know Him, you can trust Him so much more. You expect His goodness, and you expect Him to show up. We cannot function to our fullest in any capacity until we walk in healing and Sonship. As we grow in the Daddy-Child relationship with God, God will be able to partner with us to impart life to every situation we encounter. How awesome will the Body of Christ be when we all have the revelation of Sonship and see God as Daddy. WHAT A FORCE! Whatever position you need to fill in your life, let God fill it. Whether it be a father, mother, husband, or friend. Perhaps it's all of these positions. God will fill all the voids. The greater your need, the greater the measure of grace that will be given to you.

In the book of Isaiah, the prophet tells of a Savior, a Messiah, coming in chapter 53 verse 10.

> *"Yet it was the LORD's will to crush him and cause him to suffer, and though the LORD makes his life a guilt offering, he will see his offspring and prolong his days, and the will of the LORD will prosper in his hand."* NIV

Merriam-Webster's definition of the word "**adoption,**" is to take by choice into a relationship, especially to take voluntarily as one's own child.

> *"For you did not receive a spirit that makes you a slave again to fear, but you received the Spirit of sonship. And by him we cry, "Abba, Father."* ~ Romans 8:15 NIV

When someone is adopted, the parent takes on the full responsibility for the child, physically, emotionally, and spiritually. It is a transfer from one to another. Adoption means a parent sees the child as their own. Jesus is the signature on our adoption papers. However, it is so sad that many in the Body of Christ have received the adoption papers from Almighty God the Father by accepting His Son Jesus as Savior, but they choose to live as orphans. They think they are not good enough or they'll never measure up to His standards. Inferiority and intimidation, which are learned thought patterns, come against your identity in Christ and will try to inhibit the inheritance that is rightfully yours, through the name of Jesus Christ.

A friend of mine who had fulfilled the requirements of the state to become a foster parent was eligible to adopt. She was so excited when the process was complete to begin fostering with the goal of adoption. She and her husband were chosen to care for a young girl for about 6 months. The court wanted to make sure her family was a good fit for her. This family did everything they could to accommodate the girl and wanted her to feel at home. They were just ecstatic about the upcoming adoption!

While fostering her, with the intent of adoption, the girl underwent counseling to determine when she would be emotionally ready to be adopted by my friend and her family. The counselor determined she was not. In fact, it was determined that she might never get to that point with them. The foster child knew this family could give her what she never had physically and emotionally, but she told her foster mother that she didn't want to be adopted by her or anyone else. She did not want to be under the authority of anyone because she was choosing to wait for her biological mother. And because we cannot change the heart of another, a decision was made by the case workers to remove the girl from their care.

There are many in the Body of Christ that are going through life as orphans. They are Christians, but they are waiting for another person to heal so that they can receive healing just as this little girl did. She had been subjected to so much rejection and fear that it prevented her from receiving a life altering blessing. Many times we respond to what

Jesus did for us based on the wounds within. An orphan mindset also keeps us separated from our sisters in the faith. When we have not allowed God to heal us, we can react with jealousy because we have not come to understand God loves each of us perfectly and individually.

Can I urge you to believe that as a child of God, you have inherited a freedom which God has already prepared for you? Just like the young girl, who had a new home prepared for her, God has prepared a new place for you. But, the great news is that you do not have to wait to receive it!! You can walk in that freedom now.

As children of God, we have been given an exchange. We can have everything that belongs to Him, if we only receive it. He gave us the right to it by His very own life. Although we have the right to this great inheritance, if we do not believe it is ours, we will never receive it. How can a gift be utilized if it is never received? Most of our problems are found in not understanding our legal right as off springs of faith.

It takes faith to accept the blood of Jesus that paid for our sins. It takes faith to believe you will go to Heaven when you leave this earth because of His blood. It takes faith to believe you have received a new lineage, a new inheritance by a new Father. It is only by the blood of Jesus that we have been transferred from darkness into light. No other blood was worthy to defeat sin. Only the blood of God was pure and Holy to give us the remission of our sins.

Holy: without blemish

> *"In fact, the law requires that nearly everything be cleansed with blood, and without the shedding of blood there is no forgiveness."* ~ Hebrews 9:22 NIV

If Jesus had never come to serve and shed His blood, we would never be able to be called daughters of God. It is only because of the blood of Jesus that we are His children and that we can be true daughters. The

Holy Spirit gives us this revelation. It is because Jesus Christ accepted the mission to be persecuted, beaten beyond recognition, and crucified. This public display of torture revealed a public display of His great Love.

Since a seed produces after its own kind, when you received faith to receive salvation through the gift of Jesus Christ, you automatically received a great exchange. The role in which an earthly father cares for his child was given to Father God. By accepting His Son, you received God, the Father, to fulfill the mandate to care for you and provide for you. He assumed the legal position as your Father. By faith, you received Heaven's inheritance for every need to be supplied.

So, perhaps you are waiting for your marriage to change, waiting to hear you are loved, waiting to feel valued or appreciated, waiting for tenderness and intimacy from another, or waiting to be married. There are many scenarios, but whatever you are waiting for, God desires for you to come to Him right now, just the way that you are. No longer waiting for circumstances to change. He will transform you so that you can become your best you. As you seek Him to become all that you need, He will fill you and do a mighty work, fulfilling all of your desires.

> *"For everyone has sinned; we all fall short of God's glorious standard."* ~ Romans 3:23 NLT

The Lord has paid for us to become heirs of His Kingdom. Someone who inherits a gift does not have to work for it. They received the gift another worked for. We aren't to wait until we go to Heaven to receive this gift that God has given us. Right before taking His last breath on the cross, Jesus said, "IT IS FINISHED." When the Lord Jesus taught His disciples to pray in Matthew chapter 6:10, He prayed, *"Your Kingdom come, Your will be done, on earth, as it is in Heaven."*

That means you are no longer a slave to your past circumstances or the identities people have put on you. You have been given the opportunity to walk in the inheritance of the Kingdom of God. Wouldn't it be sad if you arrived in Heaven, only to realize that you had not received all of the inheritance God came to give you here on earth? When you receive His gifts, you can give to others.

Imagine this scenario, you walked with God before you were conceived. When you were born, your memory of this was erased, but inside of you has always been this deep longing for your Heavenly Father. He wanted you to come to Him without force, so He gave you free will. As a child, you had the Spirit of God living inside of you until you chose to sin intentionally, around 7 or 8 years old. The enemy, satan, did everything he could to keep you from knowing who you really were. He built a wall with offense, hurt, rebelliousness and so many other conniving ways. BUT, GOD---

He sent His Holy Spirit to draw you back. He said "No she is mine." So, He softened your heart, He called your name, and set up the atmosphere for you to invite Him into your heart and into your life. He is asking you today, "Will you come closer into the life that I have created for you? Will you let go of your life in exchange for mine? Will you lay down all of your past, present, and future, so that I can trade your limitations for My grace, which provides extraordinary power to go exceedingly above all that you can imagine or even think? Because, in My life, I provide abundant living."

God is looking for those who will love Him with their lives, who lay down their expectations, their will, their strategies, their plans, and trust that His ways are higher and much better. However, when someone has been violated, hurt, betrayed, rejected, and is still in shame, it is very difficult, if not impossible to "lay down." Laying down is a very vulnerable position. As you continue to draw intimacy in your relationship with our Great and Awesome God, you will realize you can trust Him enough that you can completely surrender and "lay down."

Look at David in Psalm 23:1, *"The Lord is my shepherd, I lack nothing. He makes me lie down in green pastures."* When we allow God to become our Shepherd in all things, we lack nothing. Not emotionally, physically, or spiritually. When we can't rest, it is because we have stopped allowing Him to shepherd us.

Ephesians 1:5 says, *"God decided in advance to adopt us into his own family by bringing us to Himself through Jesus Christ. This is what He wanted to do, and it gave him great pleasure."* NLT

Romans 8:29-30 says, *"For those God foreknew He also predestined to be conformed to the likeness of His Son, that He might be the firstborn among many brothers and sisters. And those He predestined, He also called; those He called, He also justified; those He justified, He also glorified."* NIV

God knew us before we were conceived, and He predestined us to be conformed as His children. He has called us. He has predestined our righteousness through Jesus Christ, and He has already esteemed all that we need in order to have this amazing transformation

It does not matter if you were welcomed into this world or not, YOU WERE PLANNED! Before you were conceived, you were thought of. What you would look like, your talents/gifts, even the location where you would live was all planned by God. You have purpose! The reason for your creation was simply because the Creator wants to love you and wants you to love Him in return by your own free will.

> *"The word of the Lord came to me, saying, 'Before I formed you in the womb I knew you, before you were born I set you apart; I appointed you as a prophet to the nations.'"*
> ~ Jeremiah 1:4-5 NIV

God told Jeremiah that He knew him before he was conceived and before he was born God knew what his purposes were. He knew what he had called Jeremiah for. God knew *you* before you were conceived, and He knew what he appointed you for. Your gifts, talents, appearance, and place of birth—they are all to support the call He has set you apart for. You are called to be set apart, and shine with the Son, because God lives in you and has given you everything you need.

> *"The Lord appeared to us in the past, saying: 'I have loved you with an everlasting love; I have drawn you with loving-kindness.'"* ~ Jeremiah 31:3 NIV

> *"Are you so foolish? After beginning by means of the Spirit, are you now trying to finish by means of the flesh?"* ~ Galatians 3:3 NIV

When you truly know who you are as a daughter of the KING, you become so aware of your position that not even your circumstances can persuade you otherwise. When you are certain of His character, you become so certain that He is good at all times, you long to stay under His shelter. When you cling to the Vine, which is Jesus, you will recognize the strategies of satan when they arrive. You will be so engulfed in the Kingdom that it'll be like recognizing the smell of gasoline. You won't want to consume its poison. If we do not have a full understanding of the true character of our Father, His Son, and the Holy Spirit, we will not understand Kingdom principles or Kingdom authority.

Many Christians have experienced awesome encounters with Jesus Christ, but haven't encountered the Father. Without knowing the Father, we respond in our faith like orphans, not truly submerged in the truth of His devotion and Love for His children. The Word of God is extremely strategic in exposing the roots that try to undermine us from receiving the blessings that have already been paid for by God. When you know your KING and His heart, you understand His goodness, mercy, and love triumphs over any situation. If you understand His character and the depths of His love, nothing will keep you from receiving His very best.

It is my greatest desire and the desire of the Father for you to expect His best in every detail of your life. However, how can we expect God's best when we don't recognize the counterfeit when it arrives? How can we know God is good, when we have not recognized Him as good? How can we see Him as a loving Father, if we have only experienced love with conditions, harshness, and coldness?

God is more than able, and desires to complete the healing process in you. He desires to reveal to you His goodness, His faithfulness, His long suffering, His mercy, His goodness. Think about this, if God wants you to make disciples (Matthew 28:19), how could you share with others until you have experienced Him? How can you share Him as healer if you had not experienced His healing? How could you share His faithfulness if you had not received His faithfulness? He wants to reveal more of who He is so that you can impart Him to others.

"But those who hope in the Lord will renew their strength.
They will soar on wings like eagles; they will run and not
grow weary, they will walk and not be faint."
~ Isaiah 40:31 NIV

Some of us were born in conditions that did not teach us how to "fly", and even less, impart good onto others. If you have felt handicapped because you weren't taught how to depend on the LORD or you were never given the allowance to "fly", the Word of God, with the power of the Holy Spirit, becomes your teacher in very profound ways. His Word and His Spirit are enough to teach you all that you need to know

Looking at my life today, one could ever tell that I have never had a mentor, or a teacher to stick by my side. God sent many types of "teachers" in my life. The "teachers" he sent my way came in many different packages. It is the promise of the Lord to teach you, mold you, and complete what He has begun in you. It is my mandate to share with you my life, in true vulnerability, so that you soar with wings like an eagle. Even when your wings have been clipped by situations and circumstances, He will resurrect you a new set.

Because of my great disappointments in others, trusting God came with great difficulty for me. I did not realize that all of my freedom was wrapped in my level of intimacy with God. When you are emotionally intimate with God, you allow Him to reveal hidden places that you have held onto, knowingly and unknowingly. As a result, He reveals Himself, and He always reveals Himself as Good. As He reveals Himself, He reveals who you are as He sees you one made with purpose, destiny, and power. We will never rise as His people without seeing ourselves as He sees us great victors. When we receive the revelation that we are an extension of Him, because of His great love, we will walk in great confidence that transforms everything.

Do you want your home, family, marriage, workplace, relationships, etc., transformed? The transformational power lies within you, but it begins with you saying "YES!" Your transformation is wrapped in your "yes" and revelation of your identity in Him. YOU are the seed God wants to use to produce a very healthy, and thriving garden. Will you become the seed to produce more than you can imagine? It is time for you, your gifts, and your great God-given potential to come out of hiding, so that you can soar like an eagle, the way God intended you to.

There are so many distractions that come to keep us from the intimacy our Father craves when He sees you and when He sees me. Many times as women, we put so many constraints on ourselves. Sometimes, we allow others to put constraints on us. "I HAVE to do this." "I HAVE to do that." "I HAVE to fulfill this particular obligation." "I HAVE to dust the furniture TODAY," etc. (I'm not saying it's okay to have a messy house. I'm just saying you have to have priorities). When we try to cross all our t's and dot all our i's and think our performance can bring blessings, peace, or happiness, it puts us in a bondage that strangles our joy and the freedom the blood of Jesus paid for.

Recognize the slavery of today, which God came to redeem you from. You do not need to say "Yes" to everything, even if it is something you can do. It is important that we ask the Lord what He would have us do. Sometimes as little girls, we became so good at pleasing others, that as adults, we live as if someone is still peering over our shoulders in judgement.

Don't let anything cause you to chase to and fro, from one assignment to another and another, feeling driven to constantly appease everyone. No matter what you try, and how much you work, you won't make everyone happy. It's not within your power to do so. Not even God can do that! We each choose the life we lead. You aren't called to give to everywhere and everyone. Many Christian women go from study to study, conference to conference, but fail at "pastoring" their home, the place where God has called them to serve first. You can become a slave to even good things.

Learn to rest in the assurance of His character. So many times when our prayers go seemingly unanswered, we feel as if we've missed God. We get caught up with the overwhelming long checklists of what we think we should have done. Instead of getting so caught up with distractions, rest in Him, and He will lead you and complete what He began. He is the Author of your faith, He shall complete you and take you on your journey. We just have to say "YES". Sit, rest, and trust in His grace and that He is working on your behalf. Don't try to bring transformation in your own strength because it will never come. Transformation is only found in the One who holds life.

Remember to say the prayer out loud so that you can hear what you are praying.

Father, in the name of Jesus, I give You the position as Father, Daddy. Take me on a journey to discover the adventure of knowing You have chosen me with an everlasting love. I give You full permission to love me, claim me as Your own, correct me, and teach me Your ways. I submit myself to Your authority. Help me to know You are good, faithful, loving, merciful, and kind and that You have wonderful plans for my life. Give me the courage to trust You and open my eyes to Your unfailing love for me. Help me take the seeds of love You give me and give to others what I have received. I believe You are increasing my understanding of who You are and removing the residue from my past disappointments so that I can live in freedom. I believe You love me enough to do it. Take me on a journey to know You as Daddy God, and unveil the purposes You have for my life. In Jesus name, Amen.

Write down anything you feel takes you away from a life of faith. Write down any personal thoughts or anything the Lord might have spoken to you from this chapter.

_____

_____

_____

_____

_____

_____

_____

_____

_____

_____

_____

_____

_____

—Chapter 3—

Exposing and Uprooting the Weeds of Your Soul

There are circumstances we have held onto unknowingly. Situations that traumatized our soul, or became our influence of response, or false sense of protection. Because our soul is our mind, will and emotions, whatever is flowing from our mind, will, and emotions will reflect the condition of our soul. For example, frustration from your emotions will reflect frustration from your soul.

Many sicknesses and physical conditions are caused by our soul crying out for God's resurrecting power. In order to come in contact with resurrection, you must be willing to become vulnerable with the LORD in order for the situation to lose its grip and power and be put to death. There is only resurrection in crucifixion. Now, God is not calling us to get on the cross. That was done once and for all and dealt with, but He is calling us to crucify our flesh so that we walk in His resurrection. Crucifying our flesh commands vulnerability and humility, but always leads to resurrecting power, which gives authority, and most of all, life.

None of us walk in a complete state of healing without having to continuously address the condition of our heart. Because we live in this fallen world, we need to make sure nothing has left a residue, whether it be unforgiveness, offense from people or situations. Even those we cannot recall in our mind, may have caused contamination to our soul. Now, not all of you will have stories like mine, filled with pain and darkness. But in some form, all of us have been wounded, and these wounds have caused a pattern in our lives without our recognition.

This book is not about wounds. This book is the framework that God used to transform my life from one that was utterly and shamefully broken, because of lies built on culture, tradition, destructive generational thought patterns, to a life of resurrection, grace, and love. A resurrected life is the living proof that He lives. Whether you are a little wounded or very wounded, or you don't think you are wounded at all, this material will expose your condition by gently walking you through climbing over walls that have prevented you from going forward.

In order to mature to the next level, in any context, you must conquer the level in which you are standing. All of my upbringing and into my thirties, I struggled with thoughts of perversion. I had an idea of where the root of perverted thoughts had come from in my life, and I suppose I always knew, but was too afraid to seek the answer. God, in His grace, waited until I was ready, and that is what He will do in your life, too. If you are not prepared to know the truths to release pain, He will wait until you are ready. If you are concerned with recalling information that you aren't ready to deal with, please let me encourage you. The Holy Spirit is so amazing because He is so gentle and kind. He will not reveal anything to you that you cannot handle or are not prepared for. As a matter of fact, truths are revealed slowly, in the form of a process. He will, however, use the seeds you obtain in this book, and at the appointed time, He will be able to draw from them and continue you on your journey towards freedom.

A traumatic incident is like a bad seed that produces a terrible tree that has many branches. The dark, bad tree will continue to produce poisonous fruit until you deal with the seed that produced the tree. For instance, the pornography that I found at age 4 was the seed, the rape I endured was the tree. But, it produced many branches such as an unhealthy focus on the opinions of men towards me.

Whenever the Lord has revealed a truth in my life, it has produced a deep revelation inside of me of how greatly He loves and how great He wants all of His people freed so that we can stand in our position as Son/Daughter of the KING. The more He heals you, the more you fall in love with Him. The more you allow Him to touch, the more you walk in resurrecting power. God takes us on a journey to uncover the wounds so that He can apply His love and tenderness to the very places satan wants to use as a door to come and wreak havoc in our lives. When our souls are wounded, they are very much like a door for satan to walk right in and bring more pain and destruction. It is only those things we bring to the altar of God that can be put on the cross and come face to face with the power of God, so that we can walk in resurrection. God can bolt the doors satan uses, so that you can walk in freedom in every level in your life. All you need to do is ask Him and allow Him to do it.

It is only those things that HE has revealed that can no longer stay hidden in the dark. Imagine being a prisoner who has been held captive in the dark for years that is blinded by the light. While the prisoner remained in the dark, he may not have recognized how dark it was because he became acclimated to it. But, when he got into the light, he recognized the depth of the darkness. The truth exposed is like the "light" being turned on. When the truth is revealed, it may cause us to pull back a little. You may not even recognize you were so hidden in the dark until the lights turn on, but in due time, you will experience a freedom you didn't even know was possible. It is my great expectation that the Great Holy Spirit will reveal truths to you, and the Lord's ministering angels will minister to you as you read.

Every soldier must face preparation before war. Every war comes with a battle plan because every enemy targets their enemy's weaknesses. It is time for our weaknesses to be unveiled by the power of the Holy Spirit so that we become stronger, uncontainable, and unshakeable because we walk in resurrection by the power of the blood of Jesus.

Unless we allow the resurrection of the cross to come in contact with all that has wounded us, we stand defeated. It is only that which has touched the Truth that can be set free.

The Word of God is strategic to expose roots that could undermine His blessings that He has already prepared for His people, through Jesus Christ. God left a blueprint for us to do as He instructed Adam and Eve—to multiply and take dominion. I was multiplying chaos, emotional dysfunction, and was not taking dominion over anything, because I needed to allow God to deal with the present state of my heart's soil. The tactics of satan have not changed he continues with the same strategy he used in the garden with Eve, to twist the Word of the Lord using partial truth.

Isn't it ironic that satan showed up in the garden? A place where fruit and food grows? It is the scheme of satan to show up in your "garden", so that your fruit and the food your soul thrives on would become defiled and corrupted. The lies he tells seem true. They *feel* true, and sound true, therefore we consume the lie, which, in turn, corrupts the contents in our garden.

Our garden is our life. In order to multiply anything, you must know you have something in your care. In order to take dominion, you must not only know it is yours, but know you are called to subdue, take ownership and increase it. In order to subdue it, you must put it under your authority, and one can never have authority without being under the true authority which is found in Christ Jesus. In other words, in order to increase and multiply, we must take control over the "things" we want to multiply. Since a seed produces after its own kind, the LORD, truly wants to purify His seeds (His people) so that what is produced is worthy of producing.

"Who shall separate us from the love of Christ? [shall] tribulation, or distress, or persecution, or famine, or nakedness, or peril, or sword? As it is written, For your sake we are killed

all the day long; we are accounted as sheep for the slaughter. Yet, in all these things we are more than conquerors through him that loved us. For I am persuaded, that neither death, nor life, nor angels, nor principalities, nor powers, nor things present, nor things to come, Nor height, nor depth, nor any other creature, shall be able to separate us from the love of God, which is in Christ Jesus our Lord." ~ Romans 8:35-39 NKJV

Strong's Concordance defines these as such:

Tribulation: *pressure*, especially *internal pressure* that causes someone to feel confined (restricted, "without options").

Distress: a narrow space, great distress, anguish.

Persecution: ("*religious* persecution") literally refers to those seeking to *punish God's messengers with a vengeance*

Famine: hunger **Peril:** danger

The enemy (satan) uses these exact situations to tempt us to question the love of Christ. Since I did not know the distortion the enemy had caused in my mind from consuming lies I did not know were lies, I felt separated from the love of Christ. The enemy knows the Word of God and will use these exact situations mentioned in Romans 8:35- 39 to make us feel separated from the love of God. If these situations could not make us feel separated from the love of Christ, why would they be mentioned?

When you have endured times of great pressure, great distress, persecuted by those you love, been hungry emotionally, spiritually, or physically, or had someone use weapons and hate against you, it is very easy to question the love of Christ. During these times, we become easy targets for satan, whose strategy is to cause us to believe we are separated from Love. When truth is revealed to the root system of the "garden" in our hearts, our faith and intimacy with God become ignited.

I believe that as the Holy Spirit takes you on this journey, using this book as a tool, the lies that have been seeded in your heart will be uprooted and you will experience a new level of freedom, with evidence of how you will unashamedly rise as His daughter. You will have a clearer understanding of why you respond to situations the way you do and get to the source and the lies behind them so you no longer consume them.

> *"There is therefore now no condemnation to those who are in Christ Jesus, who DO NOT WALK according to the flesh, but according to the Spirit."* ~ Romans 8:1 NKJV (emphasis added)

We will never be good enough. Praise God for the blood of Jesus! Many times I've asked God to give me grace to be able to give grace to myself. The lies that try to take you from the revelation of the love that is in Christ Jesus will be exposed in a way you can handle because the Holy Spirit is the One that will gently guide you to the truth. Truth will always set us free. John 8:32 says, *"Then you will know the truth, and the truth will set you free."*

You must be willing to seek the truth, and when you are finally at a place of trust in God and wanting to know the truth, He will reveal to you as He needs to in order for you to obtain new levels of freedom. As we allow God to have the seeds that have remained sheltered and hidden, we will allow the LORD to literally love them out of the soil of our heart so they stop producing bad fruit that continues to wreck our lives.

I lived a long, long time as a Christian in an emotional raging storm because I was resentful of my past. My marriage suffered, my children suffered, and I reacted to my present life with the wounds of my past. When we have wounds in our souls, our minds may block them, but our souls will remember until we deal with them. As an example, our bodies have memories too.

If a young athlete stops exercising, the moment he or she begins again, the muscles form quickly in the same areas they were before. My friend was a ballet dancer for many years as a child and adolescent. She stopped exercising regularly in college and resumed in her 40's. Her legs were the first area to be muscular again, in the very places they were when she was a ballet dancer. Unless we allow Jesus Christ to heal our soul, we will react according to our past. Because again, our soul is our mind, our will, and our emotions. In other words, if there are still wounds in the soul, our mind will react to our present lives based on still being conformed to its past hurts. Our emotions will reflect our past wounds. It is the desire of Jesus Christ for us to receive and utilize what He paid for.

> *"The thief comes only to steal and kill and destroy; I have come that they may have life, and have it to the full."* ~ John 10:10 NIV

If we do not deal with the bad roots within us, then we will never have the abundant life God paid for. We have to heal inwardly before it shows outwardly. It is so easy to pretend in our workplaces and for our church friends and everyone else that we have it all together. However, the real truth of our condition is always exposed to those we live with or those that are closest to us. If those we are most intimately involved with, do not see us the way we say we are, then we are in denial. Those that are closest to us are worth us walking in His healing in every way. We are worth us walking in His healing. Because otherwise, our actions are declaring that we did not receive the gifts of freedom, power, and authority in abundance. IT IS TIME! Receive your FULL inheritance through the gift of Jesus Christ from your Father God.

It is time to stop chasing things and people in order to mask the pain inside of our souls. In John chapter 4, Jesus comes face to face with a woman, a Samaritan. Samaritans and Jews were not friends. In fact, they didn't associate with each other. However, Jesus overlooked the "rules", because of His love. Jesus engaged the woman by asking her for a drink. She was taken aback that He would even speak to her, let alone ask her for a drink of water. Jesus saw someone who needed her thirst quenched, the type of quenching only He could provide. Uninhibitedly, Jesus wanted her to know that all she had been chasing was found in Him.

> *"Jesus answered, 'Everyone who drinks this water will be thirsty again, but whoever drinks the water I give them will never thirst. Indeed, the water I give them will become in them a spring of water welling up to eternal life. The woman said to him, Sir, give me this water so that I won't get thirsty and have to keep coming here to draw water. He told her, Go, call your husband and come back. I have no husband, she replied. Jesus said to her, You are right when you say you have no husband. The fact is, you have had five husbands, and the man you now have is not your husband. What you have just said is quite true.'"* ~ John 4:13-18 NIV

Jesus wanted to pierce through the masks and go straight to the reason she was left thirsty. Deep inside of her, she was looking for a love she had not found. She had married five times, and was still searching for love. He wasn't exposing her sin to make her feel ashamed. He was exposing the condition of her heart to let her know He was all she was looking for, the One who could fill her heart with all that she needed, quenching the thirst she still had. What are you still searching for? What do you run to in order to fill your needs of satisfaction? Like this woman, many women can't be alone. They search for someone, anyone to cover the pain. We search after people, positions, and objects, when all along, our soul is crying out to be touched and quenched by the hand of Lord Jesus Christ.

Since satan wants to sabotage our lives, we must de-weed any of the seeds he has planted within us. We need to uproot those seeds. In order to uproot them, we must know they are there. Once they are uprooted, we have to continue to tend to the garden of our heart so that other destructive seeds do not get planted. In the next chapter, I will be very raw and vulnerable, so that you can understand what God can do when we are vulnerable with Him, allowing Him, the Great Surgeon, to perform surgery within us. You are worth living to life's fullest potential... Free!

Remember to say the prayer out loud so that you can hear what you are praying.

Father, thank You for dealing with the condition of my heart, exposing weeds that do not belong within me. I lean to You to till the soil within my heart. Holy Spirit, I trust You will not reveal anything that I am not prepared for, and I trust You have begun the process of exposure towards my full freedom. I believe You will complete the process of healing so that the doors within my heart will be bolted and not give satan access. I recognize there is nothing that can separate me from Your love, and I depend on You. I no longer want to utilize anything that masks my pain, and I invite You on this journey so that I am made whole, healed, and free. You are my Living Water - let me come to You instead of chasing anything else, because, I want to become my best me and live to Your greatest potential. In Jesus name, Amen.

Write down all the things that you use to "mask" the pain in your soul and allow God to take what you have chased in the past and receive His grace instead. With His grace what seemed impossible before will become possible.

_____

_____

_____

_____

_____

_____

_____

_____

_____

_____

_____

—Chapter 4—

It's Time to LET GO!

If you could see a glimpse of my past, it would be a confirmation that God still heals and delivers today. Our freedom and healing is a testament of His goodness, grace, mercy, and unconditional love. Therefore, He wants to continue to reveal Himself to you. Your life is like His walking brochure. Let Him continue to "advertise" His character and goodness through your life. In order to do that, you must experience Him on greater levels, going from glory to glory, encounter to encounter, testimony to testimony.

> *"And so we know and rely on the love God has for us. God is love. Whoever lives in love lives in God, and God in Him." ~1* John 4:16 NIV

Whoever does not live in God cannot love. Although people may say they belong to God, know God, and even are led by God, the truth is, if people are not living as a testament to the Love they have received, there is no confirmation that He lives in them. Recognizing love in someone is to recognize He lives in them, and without it, there is no confirmation of what we say. How well one knows God determines how much one loves. In order to give love, you must have received and encountered His awesome love. It is not a matter of whether you *deserved* to be loved. It's a matter of understanding that people cannot give what they have never encountered. Without experiencing the true agape love of God, one cannot give it.

> *"There is no fear in love (GOD). But perfect love (GOD) drives out fear, because fear has to do with punishment. The one who*

fears is not made perfect in love (GOD)." ~ 1 John 4:18 NIV (emphasis added)

If you are still in fear as to how provision will come, of a medical condition, of your children's salvation, today's economy, or about any situation or condition, you have not allowed God to love the fear out of you. If you are in fear, in any respect, it is because you have not come to the place of understanding of God and His character. He loves you enough to bring you through any situation. God loves you so much! He really does!

In my experience, when I am still in fear about something, God loves me enough to expose that I am operating in fear, so that I can allow Him to cover the fear with the faith that I am loved. If I can just get to a place where I can receive His perspective and allow His love to bind me, I will be able to press on in faith, because I received His love.

When we understand His love in greater and greater measures as He reveals it to us, we will have no more hindrances, no more devices that satan could use to keep us from receiving ALL that the blood of Jesus Christ paid for. Every single bit! No matter what is going on, my prayer is that you would hold on to this revelation: **You are so loved and so sought after by God Himself.** When you grab hold of this truth, you will be able to become a fountain for the Lord, a source of supply to lead others to Him and His great love. You may not understand how God will resolve your issues, but if you can understand He loves you enough to resolve them, you will be able to walk through the process with increased elevations of victories. So many times the whip in the hands of those things that keep us bound to a mindset of slavery, prevents us from understanding the plain truth of the foundational Gospel.... "And God so loved, He gave" (John 3:16). GOD LOVES SO MUCH THAT HE GIVES.

This is my story of where God brought me from and how He reversed my past issues with my earthly father. It is difficult to see God as trusting, faithful, good, and loving, when we are still holding onto disappointments from the relationships we had with our earthly father. I share my story in the hope that if you have father issues like I did, you will use my story as an example of how the Lord can heal you as well, so that you have nothing obstructing your "blessing pipes". My story is only told for the purpose of revealing the great things God does for any person, no matter their background, to prove He is LOVE.

No matter how much we talk to God, if we do not understand and comprehend His character, we will miss what He has predestined for us to have. Since I did not know the character of God, I did not know how to fight back. He is calling you to know how to fight.

My mother, born a devout Catholic, became pregnant with me in the early 1970's when she was 18 years old. My father was 17 and also born in a very strict Catholic family. During the time when having children out of wedlock was shameful, my father was quite brave to take on the responsibility, even though he faced much disappointment. My mother's father was not active in her life, which caused her to become vulnerable. Before my parents got married, she was already receiving abuse from her then boyfriend, my father.

My father had many goals, but they were hidden in the secret places of his heart as he worked several jobs in order to care for his young pregnant wife. A lie that I was a mistake, that I had messed up their plans, was spoken over me when I was still in my mother's womb. My father felt like the black sheep of the family as his brothers and sisters were successful in their careers and had nice homes and vehicles. My father escaped his reality of responsibilities with alcohol, and my earliest childhood memories are filled with violence and hatred.

I grew up in a neighborhood where it was common to hear gunshots and men hitting women. At night, I could hear children or women screaming because they were being hit. No person in our home understood how to take authority in the name of Jesus, and as a result, the demonic activity that was in the neighborhood also manifested in our home. (When satan is not stopped, he has free reign and will continue to wreak destruction until one rises as a believer in Jesus Christ and utilizes Jesus' name which holds all authority.) I can recall hearing my mother's screams, her yelling my father's name because of his rages as he violently threw something at her or hit her. I remember one time hearing my father cock his gun, threatening to kill us in the middle of the night. Not knowing when or if this would happen, falling asleep was terrifying for me.

As a young child, I would go to my room and hide in the closet, or under pillows, and blankets. I would scream and weep into my pillow, because if I made noise, my father would know I was awake, and then, I would be a target. I knew how to fake being asleep, how to perfectly allow my chest to rise and fall and breathe just right so that it appeared I was asleep. I was a master of being able to hide in the closet beneath clothing, and I still did this in my early years of marriage because of feeling a need to escape.

Because of Catechism, I knew of Jesus. In my innocence, I would cry out to Jesus, for Him to come and save me, to take me away from the only home I knew. I would imagine Him there, and I would talk to Him as I would soak my teddy bear with my tears. My room was frightening to me, but I would fall asleep talking to Jesus. He was my only source of comfort, and the only One I shared my life with. As I grew older, I recall being angry with God, not knowing why He would not come. Why would He not come and change my circumstances?

As I grew, my parents had more children, 5 total. I became a 2nd mother to them. However, I was angry and abusive to them. All of my upbringing, I was told that I was stupid, I would never do anything with my life, that I was lazy, fat, and so many other words that God has proven a lie from satan. There were burglar bars on all of the windows, and I would often imagine that I was in jail. In all actuality, I was. I was in a jail that no one seemed to care I was in. My mother learned how to change the focus of my dad's anger from her by becoming the martyr. Since I was the oldest, this made me the best candidate for the release of my father's rages.

Sometimes, the food would not be cooked according to his liking, or if I wore red lipstick, or I didn't care for the children the way I was told, I would get hit. Instead of my mom getting hit, it was me. I was angry, lonely, and orphaned in spirit. I was seventeen when my youngest sister was born, and I treated her like she was my own. One day, when she was three years old and I was twenty, my father was angry at my brother, and I was told to keep the youngest away from the scene of violence. I could not help but go and protect my younger brother. So, when I heard my dad punching my brother, I yelled at my father, begging him to stop. As I saw my father's face, I saw him look beside me, and I then realized that my youngest sister had followed me. My father's rage grew.

You see, she was the hope he had that he could be a better father to at least one of his children, but now she had seen him in one of his rages. His rage was now directed at me, and my brother was free for the moment. I will never forget that day for a number of reasons. My father screamed at me and pinned me against the wall, punching me in the stomach. I lost my air, and I tried to think of anything that would stop him. The only thing I could think of was to scream out, "I love you, why are you doing this?" I had never really told my father I loved him, and it was the only thing that I thought would make him stop hitting me. However, it made him even more angry, and he punched me again. I could not understand why it was so important to prevent the youngest child from seeing his anger and why it was okay for my youngest brother and me to experience it. Later, in my life, as I grew in the things of God, I realized that demons hate love, and it wasn't my father who hated me.

49

Shortly after that incident, I had to make the hardest decision I'd ever had to make. That was to leave my home, knowing that if I left, I would not be able to protect my brothers and sisters. If I was not there, someone else would have to fall into my place as the one who received the anger. However, as hard as this decision was, it led to the path that would begin the freedom in my life as well as my whole family.

The night I left, I woke up my sister who was four years younger. I recall her crying, begging me not to go and saying that she wanted to go with me. I cried, because I knew I could not take her. It was so difficult for me to leave her there in that place, knowing it would be more difficult for her. She didn't know what she would do without me there. I stayed with a friend and her family, whom I had known since middle school. As a result of my leaving, my parents had to come to terms with the fact that they could no longer ignore that they had a problem. My leaving forced my parents to receive counseling and admit there were issues that needed to be resolved.

Years ago, I was at a fork in the road. I was a Christian, had given my life to Jesus, but I was living a tormented life. My marriage was a disappointment to me. No matter what I did, it seemed that my husband and I were emotionally disconnected. My children were not responding to my parenting style, which was controlling.

I needed help! While praying about our home life, I asked the Lord to reveal the roots of all of what was wrong in me. The Lord revealed to me that although I believed I had forgiven my father, according to 1 John 3:18 (NIV), *"Dear children, let us not love with words or speech but with actions and in truth"*, forgiveness should be also shown in ACTION AND IN TRUTH. By not honoring my father, I was not pleasing the Lord, and I could not be free.

> *"Honor your father and your mother, so that you may live long in the land the LORD your God is giving you."* ~ Exodus 20:12 NIV

50

By God's grace, He wanted to bless me and was revealing all that was restraining my blessings. Therefore, He showed me that I had not honored my father, and I still blamed my mother for not protecting me. I realized I was still stuck as an adult with the problems of my youth. Honoring my father was a direct command from God—it didn't come with stipulations – Honor him only if he treated me well, or only if he deserved it. No, because we are responsible for our own behavior and our own actions. Despite the affliction, we are responsible for our response. I was still waiting for my earthly father to heal so that I could. I was still waiting for his love and acceptance and his endearment. This is an orphan mind-set, very much like the little girl I told you about in the previous chapter that was adoptable on paper, but emotionally, she would not receive adoption.

My revelation that I was stuck in the past came around Father's Day, and I felt the Lord leading me to give my father a Bible. My mother, who had always prayed for her husband to join her at church told me, "He will never read it". I said, "Well, he will never read it if he doesn't have one!" I followed God towards my deliverance, and my father's deliverance as well. I didn't know what honoring my father looked like, so the Lord put it in my heart to write him a letter to thank him for all that he had done in my life. That was the most difficult letter I have ever written. I asked the Holy Spirit for guidance, as I needed Him to shine light on areas I could thank my father for.

I honored him for providing for us, for never leaving when most would have, for putting his dreams aside so that we could have a warm place to sleep, for being a hard worker and instilling that in us. I released my father that day. I was no longer in a "jail cell", and grace opened the door to his. That day, I was no longer waiting for my earthly father to apologize, or reveal he loved me. I chose me. I was no longer going to wait for him to change or accept me. I was going to allow God to change ME. I realized I could no longer wait, the condition of my life depended on it.

Daddy God came to fill the needs within. I had an adoptive encounter with God and He came to take residence as my Father within my heart, and He became the One whom I call "Daddy". Daddy God said, "I will never abandon you or forsake you. I am the Father to the fatherless." He tells you the same. He will never forsake you, never abandon you. He is not a man that He can lie. Not only did the Lord reveal the roots that were causing me to remain stuck, He also revealed the heart of my father. I saw my father through the eyes of love, mercy, tenderness, and grace. I saw him through the eyes of Almighty God. Seeing situations and people through God's eyes will always bring freedom. It is a strategic plan from satan to keep you from going to the next level of freedom by preventing you from seeing people as God sees them.

Since my dad received his Father's Day gift and letter, God has exceedingly and abundantly done more than I could ask about or think. God used it as a seed in the heart of my father. My parents now attend church regularly, and my dad is the first to arise and plans his day around church each week. He takes that same Bible, the Father's Day gift from me, with him.

My mother has realized God is faithful because they have been married for over 40 years, and although much of their marriage was a hardship, God has given her a new man. Not only have both of them given their lives to Jesus Christ, but my father is now her favorite and trusted friend. I love hearing about the dates they have and how he now takes the time to go shopping with her and spends time with her in ways he never did. He honors God and has asked me to pray for his friends. My father and I have a relationship that I didn't know was possible.

The Lord has taught me how to honor my parents *continuously*. When we choose to honor, God opens our eyes to seeing the gifts He has placed within those we honor. Judgement and criticism forfeits the blessing of receiving their God given qualities and anointing. When I wrote that letter to my father, it was so difficult to write because I didn't know him. But, by honoring my father, I have come to see the wonderful gifts God has placed within him. He is extremely compassionate and generous and will give all he can to help another. He is highly protective of those he loves and will do all he can do to help his children. Even now, we live minutes away from each other, and he is always willing to help when I need him, and I love both of my parents dearly!

Sharing my story of the past is not shared to bring shame or judgement on me or my family. I share my story to prove and confirm that God transforms people, which transforms families and generations. If you choose to honor those God has called you to honor, you will not be blindsided by the enemy or fail to recognize the characteristics within them which have been "rubbed by God".

I have since learned, that for years, my mother would go into the room where I slept in my crib, get on her knees and pray for change, pleading with God to help her. The Lord answered her prayers, and He used the very seed that was in the crib to reveal to her that He did work all things together for His good. My mother held onto faith that one day my father would change, and although I would never advise a woman to stay in this type of atmosphere, she has known God to be faithful. Years ago, during a women's event, I shared my testimony and had the opportunity to honor my mother publicly on the platform for not giving up on God. It is one of my most precious memories.

My father respects me now, and tells me as I look in his eyes, that he loves me, and I can respond with true love and affection. I know he is proud of the woman that I have become, and it is only because of the relationship I have with Jesus Christ. I have a Daddy God who taught me how to honor and love. Although I honor, love, and respect my earthly father, no one can give me what God has given me, as He has made me a Daddy's girl.

Without a relationship with Jesus, none of this would have been possible. I had completely forgotten about the night my father pinned me against the wall. It wasn't until several years ago while writing in my journal about all of my frustrations in my marriage and with my parenting skills, that the Holy Spirit reminded me of it. The Lord revealed the memory of that night for my deliverance and healing. Suddenly, I had a vision of that night, when at 20 years old, my father rejected my love by punching me as he pinned me against the wall. The enemy had used it as a seed of rejection in my life.

I wept before the Lord as I recalled what happened. I wailed to the Lord and cried, "Why didn't you save me from that moment? Where were you!!?" At that moment, I saw the vision again, except this time, a little differently. As I stood there, backed up against the wall with my father punching my stomach, Jesus my Lord, was standing there, holding my hand, with tears rolling down His face. I heard, "I did save you. I carried you through. You are still standing, and it is because of Me that you are not destroyed. And it is because of Me and My love that your life and story is not over."

The Lord in His great love and mercy showed me the condition of my father, who could not give what he never had. He hadn't encountered the love and grace of God; therefore, how could he give it? By revealing this to me, compassion, love, and grace arose in my heart for my father because I saw him through the eyes of the cross. The Lord tells you the same. Whatever you have been through, no matter how hurt and isolated you have become in your pain, He has been right there. Even if you did not invite Him in, He is waiting for you. He is calling your name, and He tells you, "I did save you. I carried you through. You are not destroyed."

At times in my life, I had been very jealous of people who were close to either of their parents, but not now. I love both of my parents with endearment. If I had not encountered the love of God, it would be easy for me to be jealous of my youngest sister, who has the same set of parents, yet did not receive the same parenting style as my siblings and I did. The truth is, I am so very grateful! God in His redeeming love gave my parents another opportunity to have a relationship with one of their children that would include tenderness and trust. I am so thankful that the little baby I held as a seventeen-year-old did not have to walk the journey I did. I count it an honor that I pioneered the way for her. Even now, she and my parents are especially close. This is amazing!

It is because the love of God is inside of me that I can extend it. I had the opportunity to lead my sister to Christ and disciple her to increase her understanding of God's great love. I see my parents on a regular basis, and God has had His gracious hand extended out to us. It was not ever my father who hated me, nor my mother who could not protect me. I lived under the power of lies. The truth is my father and my mother could not give me what they had never encountered.

It is only when we receive love that we can give love. That is why without God, who is Love, we can give no true unconditional love. I was the first one in the lineage of my father's name for whom God broke the chains of the curses of spiritual poverty, anger, violence, and much more. He broke the chains of traditional religion and brought me to true intimacy with Him. Because of His grace and abundant love, we have all received a new life created in Him. A life that is no longer a slave to oppression but FREE. And the best part is, I no longer need a Daddy. Daddy God, is the BEST daddy.

There are many, many scriptures that show us that THE ALMIGHTY GOD NEVER LEAVES HIS CHILDREN: God says "I am the Father who never leaves you, will never abandon you. I am the Father to the fatherless." Here are several more scriptures as further proof:

> *"The LORD himself goes before you and will be with you; he will never leave you nor forsake you. Do not be afraid; do not be discouraged."* ~ Deuteronomy 31:8 NIV

"Keep your lives free from the love of money and be content with what you have, because God has said, "Never will I leave you; never will I forsake you." ~ Hebrews 13:5 NIV

"For the LORD your God is a merciful God; he will not abandon or destroy you or forget the covenant with your forefathers, which he confirmed to them by oath." ~ Deuteronomy 4:31 NIV

"No one will be able to stand up against you all the days of your life. As I was with Moses, so I will be with you; I will never leave you nor forsake you." ~ Joshua 1:5 NIV

"I will lead the blind by ways they have not known, along unfamiliar paths I will guide them; I will turn the darkness into light before them and make the rough places smooth. These are the things I will do; I will not forsake them." ~ Isaiah 42:16 NIV

As long as we are still waiting for someone else to heal, our healing will not come. It is my pleasure to see each of you acquire and stay in the position of victory in all circumstances. In order to do that, the next step is to LET GO! We cannot heal until we completely forgive those that have hurt and disappointed us.

Remember Ephesians 6:12 (NIV), *"For our struggle is not against flesh and blood, but against the rulers, against the authorities, against the powers of this dark world and against the spiritual forces of evil in the heavenly realms."*

The Spirit of the Lord is raising a standard against all that satan brings to your mind to obstruct your freedom. As you meditate on the Word of God, the standard is being raised in order for you to recognize the weeds that come to prevent a fruitful harvest and God's perfect will.

"A little leaven leavens the whole lump." ~ Galatians 5:9 NKJV

Leaven, (yeast); (figuratively) the *spreading influence* of what is typically *concealed*.

Leaven is generally a symbol of the spreading of the nature of *evil*. If I have a wound within my soul, it is affects my soul's mind, will, and emotions. I must get the wound healed by the Love of Jesus. In order to get rid of an infection, you must go straight to the source. Now is the time for you to take the expectations you have had on people that have brought you disappointment and grief, your resentment and pain, dreams that have not come to fruition, and the memories you wish you could change, and place them all on the altar of God. You will know what you need to let go of. The Holy Spirit will reveal it to you.

For many of us, our parents are the first on the list. However, be prepared because the Holy Spirit will likely reveal more people that He wants you to release. Your list may be very long. This is quite normal. There may be people you have completely brushed away from your remembrance that come to your heart. It is important for you to know, your level of vulnerability in the exercise at the end of this chapter is very much the key towards you moving closer to your freedom. Always remember that no human is perfect, and no one can give you what only the Almighty Father can.

If you weren't embraced like you should have been, the pain you have received has not been caused by a personal issue, it has been caused by a spiritual battle. Every one of your stories has victory attached to it, but you must choose to allow victory to come by allowing God to heal you. God can use the very things that broke you, to give you a voice. He can use those situations to create a platform to bring increase and propel you into great strength and freedom.

The Holy Spirit, who is the Great Comforter, will guide you right now as you write about those past events caused by any person or any situation that hurt you. These hurts may be small or large and the acts may have been intentional or unintentional. This written work will be seen only by yourself and God. What you are about to do is a huge leap towards living your life to the fullest.

Please write openly about your earliest and most traumatic times. The Holy Spirit will remind you of those things that may have been hidden so that you can release them to Him. It is time to tend to the condition of the soil of your heart so it can be "de-weeded". The following chapters will focus on putting good nutrition in, but we must first focus on the condition of the soil. **PLEASE DO TO NOT SKIM QUICKLY THROUGH THIS PROCESS.** In order to move forward in freedom, this process is imperative to purge what needs to be purged out of your heart.

Get a pen and plenty of paper for this exercise. Although it may be tempting to skip over this part because of time or not wanting to stir up sad feelings, let me assure you, it will be worth it. The condition of your life and those near to you will be determined by how much you let go and allow God to have. Please do this exercise for your benefit. It may be helpful to play some soft worship music while you write. I suggest Julie True, who is one of my favorite worship music singers. You can get her music on iTunes or from many other sources. If you have a favorite Christian worship band that plays soft music, (anything that won't distract you). You may even prefer no music at all and just have quiet, or you might choose to surround yourself with the sounds of nature. Please do what comes naturally to you.

Now let's begin!

1. Pray the following prayer with a receptive and open heart and know by faith that He is speaking to you.

Remember to say the prayer out loud so that you can hear what you are praying.

Father, I give my heart to You to deal with its condition. Let me remain vulnerable and allow my heart to open up to You. I will no longer stay in confusion or fear, cancelling out distractions in Your name. No more will weapons prosper in my life or my household. Open my eyes to see what You want me to see. I commit my mind, will, and emotions to You. I trust You will keep the doors closed that I am not yet prepared to handle. I will put my trust in Your great love for me because You are good. I accept Your hand, and I choose to walk with You as You unveil the mysteries that will unlock deeper realms of my freedom. I invite You, Holy Spirit, to take me on this journey to produce healing and freedom. LORD, I put all of my trust, my hope, my past, my present, and future in Your hands. In Jesus name, Amen.

2. Ask Holy Spirit these questions. Write down the details as thoroughly as possible. as it is presented to you

   a) What roots need to be exposed right now?

   b) Who do I need to forgive? Be prepared! Sometimes we need to forgive ourselves and even God.

   c) What situations in my life have left a residue on my soul?

3. Ask God to reveal to you the hearts of those involved and how He sees them through the eyes of grace and mercy. If you have had a difficult time loving yourself, ask the LORD to reveal to you just how much you are loved. Just as the writing was

important in this exercise, release and forgiveness are essential
for you to go the next step.

**Remember to say the prayer out loud so that you can hear what
you are praying.**

*Father, in the name of Jesus, I release these people and the
circumstances to You. I am not saying they are right; I am saying I can
no longer hold onto them. I release (say their names) to You. I will no
longer carry them. I ask for You to take them and reveal Your salvation
and love to them. Father, place Your loving hands on the wounds within
me. Remove the infection and cover me with Your glory. I ask for You
to take first position in My heart. I give it to You. I speak to my soul,
"Soul where you have been hurt, I speak love and resurrection power
over you in Jesus name." I break all unholy ties to my soul and say,
"Soul be well, be healed, be whole," In Jesus name, Amen. I speak to
the trauma and bad memories over my soul in Jesus name. I cancel out
fear, torment, and shame. In Jesus name. (Say your name.) _____,
I say LIVE. COME OUT OF THE HIDING PLACE AND LIVE. (See
yourself at the ages you were when the destruction came.) I see myself
at the ages I was hurt, and I say be healed, be whole, be free. I speak
life and liberty over you. Be fruitful for the LORD loves you and you
can trust Him. In Jesus name, I pray, Amen*

> *"And provide for those who grieve in Zion--to bestow on them
> a crown of beauty instead of ashes, the oil of gladness instead
> of mourning, and a garment of praise instead of a spirit of
> despair. They will be called oaks of righteousness, a planting of
> the LORD for the display of his splendor." ~* Isaiah 61:3 NIV

> *"I will not speak with you much longer, for the ruler of the
> world (satan) is coming. And he has no claim on Me [no power
> over Me nor anything that he can use against Me]; but so that
> the world may know [without any doubt] that I love the Father,
> I do exactly as the Father has commanded Me [and act in full
> agreement with Him]. Get up, let us go from here." ~* John
> 14:30-31 AMP

Remember to say the prayer out loud so that you can hear what you are praying.

Father God, You are my Daddy. Help me to have nothing in common with satan, so that he cannot use anything against me. Help me to apply Your Word and seek Your face in all that I do. Let the world be convinced of how much I love You, and I do only what You instruct me to do. Let me love what You love and hate what You hate. Help me love myself with the ability to offer grace to myself as well. Give me discernment to recognize when satan is using my mind to defeat myself. In Jesus name, Amen.

Now that this exercise is complete, imagine that you are going to lay these burdens at the cross. Jesus is waiting to take each one of these writings. Symbolically, get rid of these burdens by destroying the paper. You may want to tear it up into pieces, or throw it into a fire and celebrate by making some s'mores. Allow God to do something beautiful with the pain and sadness. Resurrection could only come *after* Jesus Christ was crucified. There are dreams, hopes, and life within you that God wants to resurrect. When I facilitated in person meetings and worked through this exercise, we've used several methods of destroying our writings depending on the leading of the Holy Spirit. We placed the writings in fire to turn to ashes, torn up the paper in pieces and thrown the pieces away, or used disintegrating paper. We imagined the paper turning into ashes... and when you allow God to have them, He will create something new and beautiful within you.

—Chapter 5—

Know Your True Enemy

If we can recognize where satan has tried to attack our lives in the past, we can recognize where he will try to attack us again. It always begins in our thought life. I am not one who studies demonic activity. I study God. Whoever and whatever we magnify will have more power in our lives. However, every sportsman knows in order to win, you must know how your opponent "plays". Submitting to God is first and most important in every spiritual battle. Although this is not a book on spiritual warfare, it is important that I prepare you. When you empty a place inside of you, like you did in the exercise in the previous chapter, you allowed God to clean you of offenses and pain. Now, you need to replace those things you surrendered with the things of God.

I want to touch on several key points of spiritual warfare so that you recognize when the enemy is trying to bring destruction to your life. If we do not understand who we fight against, we will never win. If we do not understand God's strategies, we will never rise higher. We are going to do a quick run through on some aspects of spiritual warfare. It is important to address them so that we do not continue to fall prey to satan's schemes. It is very important that you understand the "strong men", or the "tribe leaders" that drive the vehicle for an onslaught of demonic activity and the symptoms and chaos they bring, so, when they attack your life, you will recognize their presence and you can rise as a daughter of the KING and come against them, in Jesus name.

Now that you have allowed and will continue to allow the Holy Spirit to dig up negative root systems that were sabotaging your best life, it is important to address that you have to act out forgiveness to those that brought you pain. This is for you, not for them. This is so that you can rise higher, leaving no residue on your soul from situations from your past that have held you down. The Holy Spirit will reveal to you what that looks like. For me, it was writing a letter to my father. With other people, it was praying blessings for them every time they crossed my mind when satan wanted to bring offense instead.

If someone is deceased, ask the Lord what He would have you do. The main objective is to seal the work that has happened within you. Just like love is shown in action and in truth, *forgiveness* is also displayed in action and in truth, because that my friends, is love. It doesn't mean you have to welcome them back into your life, or trust them. Trust and forgiveness are two distinctly different things. To reflect that we belong to Jesus Christ, we must extend grace, mercy, and forgiveness because we have received His. When someone does not receive your forgiveness, don't worry about it. Only what God has called you to do is your responsibility. Your blessings are wrapped in your obedience, not the obedience of others. So, if you aren't fighting against people, who are you fighting against?

> *"For our struggle is not against flesh and blood, but against the rulers, against the authorities, against the powers of this dark world and against the spiritual forces of evil in the heavenly realms."* ~ Ephesians 6:12 NIV

There are chains of command in the spiritual realm, just like in a military setting. Even if you do not recognize the leaders of the "tribe", the symptoms they cause will still be evident until you recognize their existence in your life. Just like a rat leaves evidence behind, a demonic presence does as well. You can always detect when there's "a rat" by the evidence that is left behind, even if you never see the rat with your eyes. You can always detect the "tribe" and their "leaders" by the symptoms they produce in your life. Demons rarely work alone. Often times, they work together to bring oppression. In order to deal with the tribe, we must recognize the "leader" that is bringing the tribe itself.

Whatever demonic oppression has been on your life will find its way back unless you recognize it and come against it. Deliverance in its entirety is not just against the demonic activity, but it involves the renewing of our mind through the Word of God. However, it is very difficult, if not impossible, to have a mind renewed in the presence of demonic influence. This is why this chapter is absolutely necessary in the life of a believer. God has given all of His children the authority to come against these spiritual "rats".

Here is an example of how these "rats" work. When I was four, I found a pornographic magazine, and although my mother tried to help me, she did not understand these demonic spirits that I am speaking of. Later in my life and in my childhood, I played sexual games with other children and became addicted to it. Sexual perversion became a lifestyle. After being married for two years, I had an affair. People do not continue to have these types of symptoms without having something within them that needs to be healed and released. In my forties, when I was already ministering, I realized I had a thought pattern that was bringing me torment. After praying about it, I knew there were incidences in my life that I had not dealt with.

Sometimes wounds are concealed and covered. As a minister, I knew how to stand against a negative thought life with the Word of God, but I wanted to know if there was anything within me that was feeding those thoughts. Although I had been married for 18 years at this point, it seemed that my opinion of men in authority had remained the same as when I was a child. Also, when I was fixing my hair before church, I wondered if others found me attractive. Immediately, I would come against thoughts like these with the Word and rebuke it. Until one day, I asked the Lord, "Is there anything in me that needs to be dealt with?"

The Lord began a two-day journey with me in order to reveal the truth. Now, was this easy? Not a bit. Was it necessary? Definitely. He revealed to me there was an access door that satan was using that I didn't know about. There were things that were done to me that I had not dealt with because they were buried so deeply, my soul knew of them, but my mind had blocked them in order to survive and cope with the trauma.

The Lord revealed to me that finding that pornographic magazine at the age of four was the beginning of the issue of lust in my life, and the thoughts and destructive atmospheres created the perfect storm. As an adult, I recalled many areas of pain from my childhood, but there were other things I could not recall. However, their existence was evident by a negative thought pattern. The unhealthy thoughts I was having towards men, caring just a little too much of what they thought of me and how I looked in their sight, revealed I had an issue that I needed God to heal.

After much time with the Lord, He revealed I had been raped by a family relative when I was ten years old. This spiritual "rat" that had come into my life at four, had grown in authority in my life. Although I had forgotten about being raped, it was the very incident that had brought increased trauma to my soul and brought an acceleration of perversion in my life. The Lord gently guided me to the truth and revealed it to me. He also revealed the heart of the person whom satan used to bring such a horrific situation into my life. Since he was not walking with God, he was only a vessel for satan to use. The man had nothing to fight the temptation with.

After realizing I was raped at ten, everything that happened in my life afterwards made complete sense. There were times in fifth grade that I was afraid I was losing my mind. I'd hear the teacher's voice take on a horrible robotic sound, and I'd put my hands over my ears and rock in my chair. I now know it was post-traumatic stress. The reason I was able to block the memory for so long was because the man that raped me, put a knife to my face and I was threatened to never speak about it, so I pretended it never happened. I remember feeling so filthy and terrified, as I splashed cold water onto my young face and fixed my hair. I looked into the bathroom mirror and swore to myself I would forget and pretend it never took place. Since I didn't have a close relationship with my parents, it was an easy strategy from the enemy.

For years, my body would react to this person's presence with an increased heartbeat, cold sweats, and tortuous fear. For many years I didn't know why I felt this way in his presence but my soul remembered what happened. Our minds may conceal a traumatic incident for a time but the soul doesn't forget. As Holy Spirit brought the childhood rape to my memory, it seemed like a dam had been opened, as I sat there with the LORD weeping for the little girl within me that had suffered such tremendous pain. I felt the comfort of the LORD as He led me to take the painful memory to the cross. I pronounced and declared healing to my soul. It was easy to imagine myself at the age I was raped. Being a mother to three children, I wept for myself, as the little girl whose innocence was stolen by such an act of selfish violence and rage. I imagined myself at the age of ten and spoke words of healing to the little girl within me that had experienced such terrible pain.

However, when the Lord revealed the condition of the aggressor's heart to me, all I felt for him was compassion and grace. I know satan longed to continue the cycle in my life as well as my children's life, but God had intervened and stopped the cycle by calling me to come and know His heart. As a matter of fact, for years, I didn't tell anyone I was afraid of having children. I was so concerned I would do to them what was done to me. Before the rape was revealed to me, I remember hearing voices that would tell me to hurt my children. But God, His amazing love comes right through, and when we allow Him to, He transforms.

When the Holy Spirit shows us the enemy's strategies and schemes, we can detect where the enemy is trying to operate in our lives. The Lord's Word says to love your God with all of your heart, soul, and mind. All three parts of you (spirit, soul, and body) have to come to a place of receiving His love and loving Him in return. When you can love God with all that is within you, every single thing, the good and the bad, and allow Him to have every incident and experience, we can choose to love and worship Him with all that is within us and all that we have experienced. I can choose to say to the Lord, "Although I have had such horrific experiences and so much was stolen from me, I choose to love and trust You with these experiences, knowing You will restore me and all that was stolen from me" The enemy cannot come against that which you place on the altar, nor can he come against your worship.

Placing everything down on the altar and choosing to worship God with it produces healing. With everything that has happened in my life, I must love God with it by giving it to Him and allowing His love to cover those wounded places so that I walk healed. His love will drive out any wounds and use what has happened for His glory. And when I love the LORD with the things satan brought into my life, I give God the painful stories to resurrect me in those places. I choose to let God have the last word.

> *"Trust in the Lord with all your heart, and lean not to your own understanding. In all your ways, acknowledge Him, and He will direct your path."* ~ Proverbs 3:5-6 NKJV

When you recognize a thought that is keeping you in the same negative mindset, tell that thought you will not accept it as yours and rebuke it in Jesus name. If you receive a thought that takes you back to a negative thought or event, remember you have already accepted healing from God. Don't worry if it returns. Just say the same thing, *"I will not receive this thought, and I cover it with the love of God, and the message of salvation. In Jesus name."*

Then, choose to fix your thoughts on what is true, and honorable, and right, and pure, and lovely, and admirable. Think about things that are excellent and worthy of praise (Philippians 4:8). When the "rat" is no longer fed, and its source of food withers, with the authority in Jesus name, it can no longer live in you and must go elsewhere.

> *"When an impure spirit comes out of a person, it goes through arid places seeking rest and does not find it. Then it says, 'I will return to the house I left.' When it arrives, it finds the house unoccupied, swept clean and put in order. Then it goes and takes with it seven other spirits more wicked than itself, and they go in and live there. And the final condition of that person is worse than the first. That is how it will be with this wicked generation."* ~ Matthew 12:43-45 NIV

BUT, if you stay on the path to righteousness the Lord's promise holds true. Psalm 119:105 says, *"Your Word is a lamp for my feet, a light on my path."* If you keep your eyes on the Lord and His Word, He shall keep you! I am going to give you a list of the names of the leaders of some demonic "tribes". The reason being, I want you to recognize when they are operating, so that you do not stay their prey.

I refer to these as "tribe leaders" because these "leaders" often become a door for more demonic influences and attitudes. Often times these "leaders" rule other spirits and work with each other. It is common for some people, including Christians, to be under the influence of several, if not many. Being under the influence of demons and demonic possession are two different things. Demon possession cannot take place in true Christians, but being under the influence (demonic oppression) is what I am speaking of and is also very common. Many Christians do not recognize that they have been oppressed by demons all of their lives and because they don't discern this as demonic activity, they take ownership of these character traits perceiving them to be their own personalities, not realizing they have been affected by a demon that has not been exposed. Jesus Christ gave us, His followers, authority over these demonic spirits, but what we do not know and what we do not recognize can sabotage us. I am exposing these spirits because when things that have been hidden are exposed, healing can begin. Truth does set us free.

The mission of these unholy spirits is to prevent or delay the development of the believer in order to prevent them from walking in their kingdom identity and purpose. Because after all, their kingdom identity (their purpose), is a magnet for attracting souls to Jesus. Demonic oppression is very real. The more a demonic presence is entertained, the stronger it becomes. Let's stop entertaining them by the grace of God and stop agreeing with them.

Exposing these spirits is not to cause any of us fear, but to help us to take our position as daughters of God to stand firm against the schemes of satan. Use this as a guide to help you not only understand these demons and how they work, but also to expose them from your life. At the end of this chapter you can pray against them, and in the "Take Your Position Daughter Workbook" the exercises are more extensive. The exercises will help you see their influences and you can pray to disassociate yourself from them and counteract by submitting to the nature of Christ.

1. The leader "spirit of jealousy", is usually directly linked to murder, anger, and rage. When someone is constantly angry and has constant fits of rage (although anger and rage can be demonic presences), many times they are driven by jealousy. The spirit of jealousy rules over murder, anger, and rage. It is also generational (learned behaviors from childhood), rooted in pride, discontentment, bitterness and ungratefulness. Manipulation, control, rejection, spirit of lying, gossip, and inferiority are often demonic spirits that work with jealousy. When someone is under the influence of this spirit, it is difficult to have close relationships with people who are gifted in ways that perhaps may get more attention from others.

This spirit prevents the person that is oppressed from seeing themselves and others the way God sees them and prevents them from growth because they are constantly comparing and competing against others. This spirit is cunning, loves division and isolating the person from others, and can oppress leaders to prevent them from growing others. Depression feeds off of this spirit. In my understanding, those that carry this spirit do not recognize they are oppressed by this spirit, because of the spirit of pride. Pride must be dealt with first and the love of God must be accepted, because often times self-rejection and not viewing themselves through the love of God is what welcomed this gang of spirits into their lives. Accept the love of God to counteract feeling rejected. Ask Holy Spirit to show you when this came so that you can find redemption at the cross and follow the protocols in this book to get free.

2. The leader "spirit of lying" is usually directly linked to adultery, profanity, hypocrisy, exaggeration, rejection and vanity. When someone is in a lifestyle including adultery, profanity, self-exaltation, hypocrisy, or vanity, the "spirit of lying" has helped create that lifestyle. The "spirit of lying" is the leader, which can bring vast destruction, exaggerating the truth is also a symptom of this spirit. The "spirit of lying" is often times rooted by rejection. Those that are oppressed learned to lie because they wanted to be accepted. When a tongue is defiled by this spirit, the tongue will be used in other ways besides lying. The tongue will partner with evil to pervert the truth, speak words that are crude and of sexual perversion, gossip, curse, and tear down others.

I find that most people who are under this demonic gang are those that also are very critical of others. These are usually people who have a hard time being humble and vulnerable and have been under the oppression of rejection for many years, if not their whole lives. Rejection can create people who cannot be trusted. If you have been under the influence of this spirit, you must first recognize it, expose it, and repent to God for yielding to it. Ask God to cleanse your mouth, because a little lie told becomes like spiritual mold to the mouth. Many women are destroying their own homes by the mold that was brought by partnering with demonic activity. Holy Spirit leads us to speak truth, leaning on Him will also bring Wisdom to know how to speak and what to speak when speaking the truth is difficult.

3. The leader "spirit of familiarity" is linked to astrology, idolatry (including constant following of specific musicians, social media or public personas, celebrities) entertaining the dead, (speaking to a person who is no longer alive as if they were), horoscopes, fortune telling, mediums, curanderos ("healers"/witch doctors in Latino communities), playing games like the Ouja board, and making pacts or vows to demonic spirits. When people engage in these activities, they are actually entertaining demonic presences that are waiting to be engaged. This invites demonic activity, which always brings deception and destruction.

The more one entertains demonic activity, the more power they give to these spirits that only want to destroy them. "Spirit of familiarity" is very dangerous because it takes on the personality and character of whomever it needs to imitate in order to be invited and welcomed into one's life. For example, when a loved one passes, a "familiar spirit" may manifest itself as the loved one in different perspectives so that it is invited to stay. It will use the person's emotional grief in order to be welcomed, all the while the grieving loved one believes it is the one they love.

Familiar spirits can also invade homes and buildings, these spirits feel they have a right to dwell in a place because people of God have not taken authority in Jesus name. These demons are familiar with those who lived there in the past and are familiar with the territory, or are invited by the one who lives there and therefore they have named it to be theirs. Sickness, infirmity (physical, spiritual, or mental weakness), addictions (alcohol, drugs, food, habits, obsessive compulsive personalities), identity crisis, sexual identity issues, tormenting and sometimes racing thoughts, perversion/lust, detaching from loved ones, coldness towards God, night terrors, and even taking on some of the traits of that which is not theirs, are all destructive patterns of this spirit. Grief, insecurity issues, feeling lonely, seeking an identity and wanting to belong, are all doors that can be used by this spirit which brings an onslaught of other demonic activity.

4. The "spirit of perversion" is the leader that causes people to live in error, brings laziness, lust, and twists the Word of God for their benefit. When counsel among believers takes place, it is very important that we do not twist the Word of God out of context for our own personal benefit. This is why it is very important that we seek counsel from people in whom we see the fruit, or the evidence, that they are truly the people they say they are. Although we should never criticize another or judge their hearts, we are to judge one's fruit. (If an apple tree produced oranges, how would I ever believe it is truly not an orange tree?) If one says they walk with God, the proof should be found in how they live, not in what they say. Twisting God's Word out of context to continue to live the way one wants to live is evidence of being under the influence of the "spirit of perversion". Perversion is a turning away from what is good and turning to what is corrupt. Perversion is also seen in perverting

sexual pleasure that is to be enjoyed in the context of marriage between husband and wife.

Same sex relations, adultery, fornication, rape, molestation, incest, masturbation, sodomy, childhood sexual games, flirtatious personalities, sexual fantasies, seduction, lying, and unholy relationships are all destructive outcomes of this spirit. Often times this spirit works with the spirit of lying and falsehoods-pretending to be something one is not, and it also often times works with vanity, wanting to satisfy a desire because they feel empty. The spirit of perversion also works with a spirit that tries to mock God (disrespect, dishonor and imitate). This is evident when the same person who loves God is the same person who does things they know God does not want for them, but because the desire is not brought under control and they seek affection, they turn from honoring God to fulfill what they are hungry for.

The spirit of perversion (twisting of the truth) works with deception. Often those that have been hurt, violated, or looking for love, are deceived into a lifestyle of same sex relations because they feel protected, validated, and wanted. We all need to be loved and the adversary uses the weaknesses within the hearts of people to use them for his gain.

When one who says they follow Christ, but lives another life, you can be sure they are under the influence of this spirit and others spirits as well.

5. The "spirit of heaviness" is associated with grief, despair, depression, hopelessness, rejection, self-pity, and sometimes gluttony. All of these can also be demonic spirits, but not always. However, the "spirit of heaviness" will always drive them. When one has gone through a traumatic event or loss, there may be a time of mourning, but after a set time, we must

arise. Otherwise, we can actually allow ourselves to be driven by this demonic presence. Depression, anxiety, loss of joy, sickness, infirmity, isolation, hopelessness, and complaining, are all attributes of this spirit.

The focus of this spirit is to restrain the person from reflecting Jesus Christ and the resurrecting power that is within every believer. This spirit is trying to make a mockery of the work of the cross and the power of resurrection. Trauma can also birth this spirit, which is why many times a spirit that invades a life through using the door of trauma from a traumatic experience first needs to be bound and cast out in Jesus name. As long as a person is bound by this spirit, the person will never see beyond their pain. Their relationships will suffer and even their physical bodies will hurt because the tormenting thoughts that cause them to suffer are sabotaging the very life Christ came to give them. This spirit is truly a destiny killer.

6. The "spirit of whoredom" leads the "spirit of prostitution" and "idolatry" (anything placed above God and His finished work). The "spirit of whoredom" is never satisfied and is sometimes seen in people who have to buy just to buy, or in those that hoard things, never throwing anything away. When a person is in this place, fear has partnered with whoredom.

Discontentment is the seed that grows this bitter root within the person's heart. An ungrateful heart refrains this person from seeing the blessings of God. You must ask Holy Spirit to reveal to you when fear led to whoredom and destroy the root by taking it to the cross.

Prostitution doesn't just mean someone selling sex. It is chasing after addictions that come against our relationship with God. The "spirit of prostitution" can also be seen in someone who has multiple sex partners, or who has had many sexual partners.

The spirit of prostitution can also be seen in someone who has to have a partner because of feeling lonely, and having someone gives them a false sense of belonging. Perversion is often coupled with this spirit. Since this spirit is never satisfied, even when the person receives what they think they want, they are still looking for more. Addictions can oftentimes work with this spirit.

7. The "spirit of infirmity" can cause a person all kinds of sicknesses, but not all sickness is controlled by this spirit. Too often we have chosen paths that bring sickness as a consequence of not properly caring for ourselves. The spirit of infirmity means weakness of the body; physical, spiritual, or emotional. It destroys a little at a time, with one issue leading to another. Often times this spirit has been birthed through fear and/or rejection. People who have gone through traumatic experiences can be bound by this spirit. Its intent is to not only hold its victim captive, but also to destroy this person from the inside out.

Spirits of hopelessness and despair often work with this spirit, as well as self-rejection, and is birthed from listening and believing the many lies, accusations, and exaggerations of the truth that are told by the spirits to the mind of this person, which is how this spirit got in and gained ground. Without taking every thought captive to the knowledge of Christ, the person allows a full onslaught attack to their minds which is seen in the condition of their bodies. Depression, anxiety, mental illness, weakness and sickness in any of the systems in the body, partnered with past trauma, rejection and/or grief, can surely reveal the oppression from these demonic spirits. Receiving the love of God is always the antidote for healing the broken place and His healing hand can mend the darkest place when we invite Him in.

8. The "spirit of deaf and dumb" manifests itself in insanity, epilepsy, suicide, seizures, and other mental issues. I have found this spirit often, but not always, enters in the early stages of childhood through traumatic events. When one wants to escape a situation or atmosphere, many times the child will desire to be "shut off" from her world. This can cause bipolar disorder, multiple personality disorders, schizophrenia, and/or severe depression, which can turn into cutting/self-wounding, suicidal thoughts, and/or an inability to express themselves, because this spirit has bullied them and has silenced their voice. They have been convinced that their voice does not matter. The spirit of deaf and dumb is also seen in the spiritual and emotional context of not speaking up. It is often times partnered with timidity and fear, and is often birthed in atmospheres of abuse.

When parents, leaders, and/or persons of authority have misused their authority, trauma can cause a person to become "deaf and dumb", which prevents them from stating their opinion or afraid of "getting it wrong" so they don't try. Many who are oppressed by this demonic activity are also oppressed by fear, anxiety, worry, intimidation and insecurities. This spirit can gain entry when another spirit leads situations that caused them to be bullied and creates the perfect atmosphere for the spirit to be accepted. Rejection (being rejected from others and self-rejection; not liking themselves), abandonment/neglect, abuse, and trauma, often need to be dealt with alongside this spirit.

9. The "spirit of fear" includes a lot of torment, terror, worry, anxiety, timidity, inferiority complexes, and phobias. The fear I am speaking of is not the emotion "fear", but an onslaught of attack from a demonic source, including tainting one's personality for its use. Many times, this spirit has become a part

of a person's life during their childhood, and therefore, a person knows no other way of living. This spirit debilitates one's life and can also bring about insomnia and nightmares. Night terrors are also driven by this spirit, and usually brought on by trauma in one's life. This spirit greatly opposes a person's increased faith in God.

Fear uses the emotions of people to prevent them from walking in their Kingdom purpose. Being rejected, abandoned, neglected, abused or traumatized are all open doors for fear and all work together to keep the person in a web of captivity. A slavery mentality, (feeling like you have to do in order to receive), including a spirit of poverty, (feeling like you may not have enough, or holding onto something because you are afraid of not having enough, or being dependent on a system or people to give you what you need), are all destructive mindsets that have partnered with demonic spirits and allow fear to lead. Faith in Christ alone and His goodness unlocks the doors to freedom, after rejecting this spirit and removing it from using you.

10. The "spirit of pride" includes mockery, stubbornness, gossip, contentions, criticism, self-exaltation, perversion and deception. This spirit shows up with inferiority and intimidation issues as well. It hides well in one's life as this spirit makes it difficult for them to be candid or reveal their vulnerabilities, and they are often very concerned about not being respected. Usually, this spirit causes one to be *overly* boisterous and showy in their mannerisms. They seem to demand to be treated differently than others to prove their superiority, using passive aggressive behavior to demonstrate and demand they are to be respected and honored, which is to be treated differently than others. This spirit causes the person to feel a sense of entitlement. This spirit is cocky and arrogant, which prevents the person from leading people effectively to Jesus.

This spirit also hides well behind very gifted people. When things don't go their way, they can often manipulate to control through tears or any other outward reflection in order to get what they want. They don't always follow the rules, because they feel a sense of superiority. People who carry pride often bring dissension and their lives often don't have order. Often these are people who have been hurt by others, specifically those in authority over them. Often times, they do not recognize they have partnered with witchcraft because they seek to control and contort situations in their favor, and it is pride which is leading them and being rejected by others has them wanting to matter; wanting to be loved and desired.

Witchcraft is not only casting spells and tarot cards, witchcraft is also manipulating others through words and actions, praying prayers that appeal to your own agenda and not considering God's will for those you are praying about, gossiping about others and speaking badly about them and using words when you are hurting in order to hurt them in return. Witchcraft is much more extensive than this, but it is fed by pride. And pride is usually birthed through rejection. If we do not handle the places we have been rejected through our position in Christ, we will be led by the wrong spirit.

This Spirit is often generational and brings much division in families, homes, marriages, churches, and relationships. Unfortunately, ministers can fall under the influence of this spirit when they begin to try to build ministries in their own strength. This spirit wants the people of God to do things in their own strength so that their influence is limited.

11. The "spirit of bondage" manifests in fear, anguish, and addiction and causes spiritual blindness, which prevents someone from receiving spiritual truths. This spirit keeps the

eyes and ears closed from seeing Truth. They cannot see and they cannot hear. Many times, one cannot receive the Gospel until this spirit is dealt with. People who are being oppressed by this spirit will choose some parts of the Bible to follow, but cannot follow the LORD in other places because they are bound in those places within them. They can hear the LORD in some places, but not the bound place, because the bound place has authority over those aspects in their lives. For instance, if a person has no problem tithing because they trust God with their finances, but can't stop having sex outside of marriage and justify these activities, they have closed their ears and heart to the scriptures that pertain to sex outside marriage and are bound in that place.

When the "spirit of bondage" drives someone, they no longer feel as if they have any control over that place, for this spirit has stamped its presence in that place and is ruling and leading. This spirit is quite destructive because its true intent is to keep this person on a continual decline towards great despair and destruction. The spirit of bondage is on a continuous pursuit to be engaged in the sin of its choice. The person cannot get rid of the thoughts that lead to engaging in the activities that they have become dependent on. The promise for contentment is never fulfilled. It is a race that is never won. If you know it is a sin to engage in a specific activity, but you cannot stop it, you probably are dealing with a spirit of bondage.

12. The "spirit of anti-Christ" denies the deity of Jesus Christ and wants to oppose the Gospel. Even when one appears to have accepted the Gospel, this spirit wants to oppose the spiritual growth of the individual because of covenants made from past generations in his/her lineage. Doctrines of the faith are constantly challenged. Their prayer lives are constantly distracted and much opposition is given to their walk with God.

The spirit of the anti-Christ is also a spirit that has invaded the Church and people of God to prevent them from revealing their Christlikeness. The more we focus on the problems and affairs of this world and follow the entertainment of the world, the easier it is to be fooled by the spirit of anti-Christ. Marriages, homes, relationships, communities, and workplaces have anti-Christ spirits that are assigned to them to keep people of God from revealing the nature of Christ. Without recognizing them, we partner with them and miss the opportunity to see God move.

It is also important to address one of the most common things satan uses against people are lies of self-hate. Self- hate is extremely common, although many will not reveal it. When you hear thoughts of self-hate and self-destruction, (anything that tries to devalue you) whether it be your own thoughts or from the lips of others, recognize the enemy is only exposing his presence. Do not cooperate with these spirits that are trying to bring destruction to your life. You are of priceless value, uniquely and intricately made. Do not allow these spirits to have their way in your life. The enemy will not just go away because we ignore him. We must face him head on with the knowledge of Jesus Christ, (take authority in the name of Jesus put on the character of Jesus Christ). Since the enemy is a spiritual being, we cannot stand up to him in our own strength. We must face him through the One, Jesus Christ, who has already defeated him.

As we hide in the shadows of God's wings, by abiding in Him and using the tools in this book (which are biblical principles), you will see yourself overcome every situation. I also highly recommend that you get my "Take Your Position Daughter Workbook" and go through the exercises to divorce the alignment between you and unholy spirits. I will walk you through exercises and prayers to help you expose the mentality these spirits produce when they are recognized. You can find the workbook on Amazon, "Take Your Position Daughter Workbook".

Remember to say the prayer out loud so that you can hear what you are praying.

Father, in the name of Jesus, give me Your discernment to recognize when a demonic spirit is trying to operate in my life. I want to recognize what is of you and Holy and what is not. If there is anything that needs to be dealt with within me, lead me to break its presence off of my life, in Your name, so that I can grow and develop in You. Help me rise above the works of satan so that I can live life with the purpose You intended. I choose to submit to Your headship, so that I can walk in victory. Reveal to me any spirit I need to be aware of in my life as I depend on You. Holy Spirit, give me courage and boldness to stand in Your power. Help me to be aware of anytime I am agreeing with the enemy regarding myself or others so that I can break agreement and agree with You instead. Help me see myself and others through Your perfect vision. Open my eyes and heart to know You more and Your love for me so that I do not fall for a counterfeit version. I want any and all tribe leaders and the gang they brought to my life to be bound and released off of me in Jesus name. For every destructive fruit that has been produced, remove yourself and leave my life, in Jesus name. I choose You, LORD. Receive my life and all the parts that make it, and do what only You can do. Thank you for the Blood of Jesus, which paid for my freedom. In Jesus name, Amen.

—Chapter 6—

Transformed from the Inside Out

I'm very thankful that you are on your way to representing who you truly are because of your redemption by Jesus Christ. For those of you who remained open, vulnerable, and ready to allow God to expose some roots that needed uprooting in Chapter 4, God did some powerful things inside of you. (If you were not ready, and you skimmed through the chapter as quickly as you could, that is okay. In due time, God will help your heart become ready.) This book is merely a tool. He is the true Surgeon who shall complete what He has begun in you.

When God removes the poison that was causing damage, we need to fill ourselves back up with good and pure nutrition. It is very important to fill that space that which was occupied so that you will continue to move forward in the things of the Spirit of God. As you stay true to this path, I am confident that the negative cycles in your past that have tried to prevent you from fulfilling your full potential, will no longer have power over you. The Word of God says in James 4:7 (NIV), *"Submit to the Lord, resist the devil and he shall flee from you."*

The continued framework of this book is just that, a teaching on how to submit to the Lord towards a path that will keep you moving in the direction of His freedom, if you are careful to His counsel. It is the counsel God has directed me with, and since it continues to work for me, it will certainly work for you. What is God asking you to do concerning people who have hurt you? Sometimes it is only to pray for them. Sometimes it is nothing at all. Other times it is to show them an act of grace. What is HE calling you to do? Ask Him, and write your thoughts here.

_____

_____

_____

Imagine two high school classmates, one comes from money, never knowing financial hardship, the other has known financial hardship all of her life, and both of them are at Goodwill buying clothes. The one who has never experienced financial hardship is unashamed, and doesn't shopping at Goodwill negatively. The other hides. She doesn't want the other classmate to see her. To her, shopping at Goodwill is shameful. Both girls past experiences have determined their present actions and emotions. We must realize our identity is not in where we have come from- it is found in the One who paid for our eternal position. Also, it is important to recognize, that unless we have walked in another's shoes, we cannot truly empathize with them. Therefore, we should never judge why someone is having a difficult time. What is difficult for you, may not be difficult for another.

When I was a child, I always wanted name brand clothes, but me parents could never afford name brand clothing. My friends had them, but I never did. In the 80's, name brands were very common. Even in communities with low socioeconomic levels, the teenagers wanted name brand clothing, and many parents did whatever it took to get them. Having to have a name brand anything and hiding behind an image is very deceiving. It's deceiving because it seems when we receive the thing that we are wanting, joy will come, but temporary items give temporary satisfactions. It is not to say that we shouldn't want nice things, but if we base our contentment on items, **then we are still being identified with our possessions and not the One who possesses us**. If we are still trying to impress others, we are not walking healed and overcome. Although Jesus Christ was rich in every way, He gave it all up to serve His Father.

"For you know the grace of our Lord Jesus Christ, that though he was rich, yet for your sakes he became poor, so that you through his poverty might become rich." 2 Corinthians 8:9 NIV

We are all in one of three states of being: 1. A Victim 2. A Survivor or 3. An Overcomer

A victim is someone who has been injured or destroyed. A survivor continues to exist or to merely live, but this is not abundant living. An *overcomer* is **one that overcomes and has changed position from one that has been defeated, to one who defeats.** She is one who has gained control over something difficult, the very situation that tried to destroy her. Victims and survivors are still living with their past identifying them. When one overcomes, their past doesn't identify them, they identify their past. When you overcome, you are no longer ashamed of the situation that tried to hurt you, kill you, or destroy you. That situation becomes a birthing process by which you allow God to use it for His glory to benefit others. By sharing with others what we have learned and being quick to love, God can utilize our past mistakes and failures for the sake of bringing others hope and freedom.

How does someone identify their past? By not being ashamed of it, and by allowing God to take their past and make it a lesson in their journey to help others in theirs. For example, when the girl without money overcomes, she will not feel fearful, intimidated, or inferior for shopping at Goodwill. She will know that she is not defined by her bank account. As a matter of fact, she might feel confident enough to share her great bargain stores with others because she now knows who she is and whose she is.

Can you imagine how it would feel to be executed for a crime you did not commit? To be publicly chastised, with those you thought knew, who you thought loved you, just standing by without advocating for you? He, Himself, the KING of Heaven, chose to be publicly tortured and naked on a cross because of LOVE. Can you imagine the burden Jesus Christ felt in the Garden of Gethsemane knowing what would take place and the torture that was coming? In Luke 22:42, He cried, *"Father, if you are willing, take this cup from me; yet not my will, but yours be done."* He could have said NO! But, love compelled Him, and His mission on earth as the Son of God was completed. His obedience to the Father compelled Him, and His focus was the Kingdom. Although people spit in His face, their response did not determine His identity, nor did it prevent the outcome of His mission. He is GOD, our Savior, the Messiah.

In order for people to know who He was and who He is, He had to know who He was. Who are you that people may not have noticed? Who you think you are will determine your ability to focus on circumstances or those things that are eternally important. What did God place inside of you that hasn't been honored? If Jesus hadn't said, "Father, let your will be done," He would not have been crucified. If He would have run away from His identity, we would never have hope. If He had not been crucified, He would not have gone to hell in our place. If He had not gone to hell, we would never be able to go to Heaven. If He had not died, He would not have had been resurrected, and we would never know Him to be our Savior.

Perhaps people haven't seen you. Perhaps you haven't really seen yourself. But God has! I believe just as Jesus was led by the Father step by step towards His mission and victory. He leads us step by step as we allow Him to hold our hand and grow in Him. As you grow in Him, He will lead you to fulfilling for which He created you, and honor you, just like Jesus!

God has great gifts for His children, but because of His great love, He does not want the gifts having the heart of His people. When you are content in the current areas where God has blessed you, and your heart is devoted to the Lord, He will promote you. As an OVERCOMER, it is imperative that we stay grateful. For gratitude will keep our eyes on the One who blesses and not the blessing. When our eyes are on the One who blesses, no gift, or lack of gift, can steer us away from the One who heals us, keeps us healed, and gives us unimaginable peace. It is important to test the condition of our heart when we ask God for things. What is the purpose of the request? Are you being faithful with what you have in your care now?

For instance, if God gave you the house you want, would it take you away from Him and the level of intimacy He longs to have with you? Sometimes, we long for things or possessions because we feel they would validate us or cause people to applaud us. It is extremely important to ask God to search our heart so that in everything we respond from a healed perspective.

"Search me, God, and know my heart; test me and know my anxious thoughts. See if there is any offensive way in me, and lead me in the way everlasting." ~ Psalm 139:23-24 NIV

Merriam-Webster's Dictionary defines **"Identification"** as the act of finding out who someone is and revealing who they are; understanding the problems or experiences of another person: the act of identifying with someone.

In other words, our reaction to circumstances determines if we are *identifying* ourselves as either a victim, a survivor, or one who has overcome. Take a good look at yourself using the Word of God. If you could really look in the "mirror" and see how you respond when you face difficulty, when you feel jealous, or when you are afraid, what would you see? Instead of focusing on what you are *feeling,* look for the root cause. Do not dismiss it! Take a good look and search out the truth. What is it that you need? What is it that you feel you are lacking? Ask the Holy Spirit to give you whatever it is. When you do this, you are actually submitting to the Kingship of Jesus Christ, and the authority of the spirits that are trying to attack you will lose their power/restraint.

"Submit yourselves, then, to God. Resist the devil, and he will flee from you." ~ James 4:7 NIV

"Therefore, if anyone is in Christ, he/she is a new creation; the old has gone, the new has come!" ~ 2 Corinthians 5:17 NIV

Our past experiences, good or bad, will determine our present actions, unless we raise the standard of the Word to them. Our past experiences will be the source of how we relate to our present lives, unless we allow the Word to renew our soul (our mind, will, and emotions). How we identify ourselves will be revealed in the boundaries we place on ourselves and others.

Where are some areas where you personally need to be renewed? What reactions do you have that need to be conformed to the Word? Whatever those areas and those reactions are, there is freedom in submission to the Word because it is truth, and the truth sets us free. When we deny the process of becoming renewed, it is because we are not desperate enough to seek God for the answer in the Word. When will enough be enough? Perhaps God wants us to get to the place where HE is ENOUGH FOR US?

In order for us to submit to God, we may need to talk to ourselves a lot—and most of the time I say, "Monica, get over yourself!" Pretty much everything can be fixed with that line. People taking too long in line — "Monica, get over YOURSELF." People are talking about me and my choices...... "Monica, get over YOURSELF!" Sometimes, I say it so much that I hear the Holy Spirit agreeing with me. It's pretty funny to me that when I get frustrated and moody or easily irritated, I can hear the Holy Spirit say, "MONICA," and I say "Yeah, yeah, I know!" If you seek change and renewal, the Holy Spirit is ready to partner with you to coach you along the way.

> *"... And to put on the new self, created to be like God in true righteousness and holiness."* ~ Ephesians 4:24 NIV

You must have a revelation of Ephesians 4:24. The Word says *to put on* the new self. Therefore, we are given a mandate. You have to choose to PUT ON THE NEW. We can't walk in our new selves until we choose to walk out of our old selves. If I never turned on the oven before putting in the food, it would never get baked. Therefore, be cautious to always put on your new self because your old self will try to come back. Many times when it seems I cannot do something because the task seems too daunting, all I do is ask for the grace to do it. "Lord, this is too difficult for me. I ask for the grace to help me submit to Your Kingship and Your will."

What does submitting to His Kingship mean? It means instead of doing things the way you want to do them, you CHOOSE TO DO IT THE WAY HE CALLS YOU TO DO IT. Whatever that is. It's not that you feel like it, or that you even know how. But, it is saying and living in awareness that He is your King, your LORD, your God. Jesus lived this on earth and fulfilled the will of God for His life, and through the power of the Holy Spirit, it is possible for you to do the same.

There was a time in my life when inferiority was a huge issue for me. If I walked into the room without others acknowledging me, I immediately began to believe there was something wrong with me. I want to encourage you to know that when you have a thought that doesn't line up with the Word of God about you and your worth, it is the enemy exposing his identity. Since the enemy is a spirit, know that not only is he exposing his presence, but he is exposing the thoughts other people may be having in the room. If you can get to the place in your heart to ask God to see yourself and others as He sees, and ask the Lord to reveal to you who you can pour attention and love into, satan will lose at the very thing he tries to prevent you from doing— Walking in God's love.

In the book of Esther, Esther was an orphan. She had neither mother nor father. She had to learn how to be a queen. She had to give up her former ways and learn how to represent royalty. To make matters worse, she had to do it in a culture other than her own. She spent an entire year preparing before being with the king. She went through a process of purification, which is what we must do when we are transferred from darkness into light. In order to represent ourselves as daughters of the KING, we must *learn* how daughters of the King react and walk in freedom. We must know how to carry ourselves, how to think of ourselves, and how to represent the Kingdom we have become a part of. Our former ways must go, and we must put on our new identity. It doesn't come naturally, but as we seek the truth, our former ways will begin to fall away because a new process has begun.

In this session we will learn how to transform from the servant to the King's wife, "Esther." It is time for us to walk in transformational anointing.

> *"Don't be conformed to this world, but be transformed by the* **renewing** *of your mind, so that you may prove what is the good, well- pleasing, and perfect will of God."* ~ Romans 12:2 WEB

Strong's Concordance defines TRANSFORMED- **3339 as** *metamorphóō* (from 3326 */metá,* "*change after* being *with*" and 3445 */morphóō,* "changing *form*

When I think of the word transformed, I think of metamorphosis, as in when a caterpillar transforms into a butterfly. It's not the caterpillar's job to transform into a butterfly. The only two things required from the caterpillar is to consume enough nutrition and to stay in the right atmosphere in which to grow, because everything the caterpillar needs in order to be transformed is already inside of it. We are going to look at the life stages of a butterfly because it is important that you realize your growth, as the created, is the job of the Creator. You will do your part in eating the nutrition and being in atmospheres that support you, and He will do His. Whether this is where you are, or you have been praying for others who seem to not be progressing, the progress is found in the process of maturation.

The First Stage of a butterfly's life is the "egg stage." If I drew an illustration of salvation, this is what I believe it would look like. The first stage would be when we accept Jesus Christ as our Lord, and we would appear as a tiny little egg, the first glimpse of "new life." The coolest thing about butterfly eggs, especially monarch butterfly eggs, is that if you look closely enough, you can actually see the tiny caterpillar growing inside. If one looks closely at the life of a new believer, it is the tiny changes that have begun in his/her life.

The Second Stage is the larva or caterpillar- Caterpillars need to eat and eat so they can grow quickly. When a caterpillar hatches from the egg, it is extremely small, but when it starts eating, it instantly begins growing and expanding, growing and expanding. Its skin does not stretch or grow, so it grows by "molting" (shedding the outgrown skin) several times. As the caterpillar eats and grows, it sheds, in a continuous fashion. Just like when a new believer eats the Word of God, they begin to shed some habits. If a new believer wants to grow and mature, just like a caterpillar, they must eat and eat the Word of God.

As they renew their minds constantly with the Word of God, their old ways, their old identities, will start to shed. If a caterpillar stopped eating, it would not continue to grow and advance to the next stage. It is just the same with believers as they continue to grow by renewing their minds with the Word of God and growing in their relationship with God. As we increase in the Word of God by submitting to its authority, our old ways, our old identities, and our old destructive patterns will begin to shed from our lives. It is the caterpillar's job to eat in order to mature and advance.

It is our job to eat the Word as well. As we eat the Word, we must ask the Holy Spirit to illuminate the scriptures to increase our revelation and understanding. When we eat the Word of God, we must not read it like a book. We must eat smaller portions at a time, meditate on it, then chew it some more. When we do this, God can actually cause the Word to become alive. If you do not know how to digest your food, you will not receive adequate nutritional value.

The Third Stage in a butterfly's maturation is the pupa (Chrysalis)- The pupa stage is one of the most amazing stages of a butterfly's life. As soon as a caterpillar has grown and has reached its full length/weight, it forms into a chrysalis. From the outside of the chrysalis, it looks as if the caterpillar may just be resting, but it's the inside where all the action is taking place. Inside of the chrysalis, the caterpillar is rapidly changing, and extraordinary advancements are happening. Perhaps you want to do some extraordinary things in your life. Perhaps you truly want the Lord to use your life to draw people to Him. Even if it seems you are just resting, there is some remarkable work being done to your spirit as you stay in His presence.

If you have been eating the Word for some time, and it seems you are not going anywhere, know that inside of you there is a process happening, and at the appointed time, your wings will be prepared for the journey God has called you for. There are some remarkable happenings going on inside you. As you read the Word and then apply it, as you submit yourself to the Lord and His Kingship over your life, even before you or anyone else notices, your soul, mind, and emotions have begun to change.

Now, as most people know, caterpillars are short, stubby and have no wings at all. Within the chrysalis the old body parts of the caterpillar are undergoing a remarkable transformation, called metamorphosis.

Soon, the beautiful parts that make up the butterfly will emerge. There are times when it seems that in everything you do there is discomfort. It may even seem like the passion has dwindled, and you have become dissatisfied with things that at some point satisfied you. Know you are on your way to advancing into the next stage. When the time has come, and you have received adequate "training" and nutrition, and the pupa is finished, you will be ready for the final stage of a "butterfly's life cycle."

The Fourth Stage is an adult butterfly. Finally, the caterpillar has done all of its forming and changing inside the chrysalis. When the butterfly first emerges from the chrysalis, both of the wings are going to be soft and folded against its body. This is because the butterfly had to fit all of its new parts inside of the small chrysalis. Just like when we conform to our new identity, a caterpillar has been changed from the inside out. By looking at the butterfly, there is no indication whatsoever that it was once a caterpillar. This is the same for you and me. Once we have been transformed, there will be no indication whatsoever that we were wounded, nor will we resemble any part of our past life.

As soon as the butterfly has rested after coming out of the chrysalis, it will pump blood into its wings in order to get them working and flapping, so it can fly. In the same way, the Spirit of God "pumps His presence into your wings." He is your strength, in order to get your wings working and strong. The butterfly will master flying and will search for a mate in order to reproduce. When in the fourth and final stage of their transformation, adult butterflies are constantly on the look out to reproduce. When a female lays their eggs on leaves, the butterfly life cycle will start all over. The main mission of a female who is reproducing is to look for the leaves it wants her offspring to eat. Therefore, she sets up the atmosphere to make it easy for the young caterpillars to grow.

Mature daughters in Christ are always looking to reproduce by investing in the lives of others. In order to reproduce, there must be a labor process—Laboring to heal from our past—Laboring to nourish ourselves—and Laboring to love others. It is not always easy! That is why we labor for the sake of the Kingdom. But, God is always prepared to give us the grace to do it. Let's not put a "whip" to the world. Let us remember the process we have received and love others into the Kingdom of God.

It is so easy for our growth to be stunted. Many times situations that make us angry or hurt us are only strategic devices of the enemy to inject "poison" and attack our spiritual condition. We must choose life. We must choose to stay in atmospheres that strengthen us, and also be mindful of strategies set in place that try to prevent us from being a thriving "butterfly". Since diving into the material covered in this book, have you recognized the atmospheres that come against your growth? Have you been able to detect the relationships that support your spiritual growth and those that deteriorate it? It is important that you recognize these because when they are recognized, you will be able to cultivate the good ones and not be easily poisoned by the bad ones. If you can't refrain from these cycles that prevent you from growing closer to the Lord, ask Him to help you. There is nothing you can't ask of Him.

If there are some relationships God reveals to you that are not helping you, and you haven't come to the place of being strong enough to not allow the circumstances to be a stumbling block, I want to encourage you. Being daughter of the KING, does not mean you must accept every relationship. It is sometimes necessary to pull away from relatives until we are strong enough to stand against what brings us down. If there are people who pull you back to a lifestyle God has pulled you out of by telling you that you must come back to the relationship because "it is the Christian thing to do," be aware that is another tactic of the enemy. You must allow God to heal you thoroughly.

People often make the mistake of thinking they can hang out with everyone and anyone, believing they are to be a light in the darkness. It is very true that we should be a light in the darkness, but if you go back to the atmosphere, are you really being a light or are you conforming to the darkness? If you go into the darkness to be the light, then that means you are mission-minded, having the purpose of sharing the One that is the Light. Otherwise, we are only deceiving ourselves. Many times, satan twists this truth, and people go into the darkness thinking they are the light, when really they can do nothing on their own. Unless God has told you to go back to the places He pulled you out of, don't go back. You will be going on your own accord in a vulnerable state, baited by satan.

Going into the darkness as having the Light, means you do not participate in things of the dark, because dark and light have nothing in common. Whatever we represent, the Light or the dark, is the power that will be represented in our lives. As a daughter of the KING, light is a reflection of LIFE. Without the sun, there is no source of light. Represent He who is Life, because He lives in you. The Message version says it best,

> *"So here's what I want you to do, God helping you: Take your everyday, ordinary life—your sleeping, eating, going-to-work, and walking-around life—and place it before God as an offering. Embracing what God does for you is the best thing you can do for him. Don't become so well-adjusted to your culture that you fit into it without even thinking. Instead, fix your attention on God. You'll be changed from the inside out. Readily recognize what he wants from you, and quickly respond to it. Unlike the culture around you, always dragging you down to its level of immaturity, God brings the best out of you, develops well-formed maturity in you."* ~ Romans 12:2

You cannot be renewed without the presence of God, and without the Word being applied in your life.

—Chapter 7—

P.O.W.W.E.R. to Stay on Track

Here is the best news of all! Christ came to give us LIFE, and life more abundantly! The Lord took me on a journey through the process of transformation from broken and wounded and limited in power, to becoming whole, healed, and victorious in Him. He gave me six keys that has never failed to work, no matter what storms have come my way, without the need of counseling or on-going pastoral care. As you take hold of these six keys and put them to practice, it will lead you to your God given purpose and keep you walking on the path of righteousness.

The Holy Spirit gave me a wonderful acronym for staying on course for my journey as His Daughter. True Daughters of God walk in His power. We are going to use the acronym **P. O. W. W. E. R**. as a way of reminding us and helping us to stay on the right track.

In the following chapters, I will share with you 6 keys to walking in power as a daughter of the Most High God.

P- Prayer

LIVE A LIFE OF PRAYER —We have to live a lifestyle of prayer. Daughters of the KING have a strong prayer life and see the evidence in their lives because they have humbled themselves to a life of a disciplined prayer walk.

There was a time in my Christian walk where I was told that in order to have a strong prayer walk, I had to pray for several hours at a time.

But, this was daunting for me. Actually, it's wrong! Prayer is a lifestyle and doesn't belong on a checklist of chores. It is an honor to continuously fellowship with God, constantly allowing Him to tug on your heart when someone needs prayer or to have no agenda but to enjoy His presence. There are different types of prayer, but we won't get into those in this book. The type of prayer I am speaking about is one that keeps communication with God continuously and one that keeps you available to God for the needs of others.

> *"And pray in the Spirit on all occasions with all kinds of prayers and requests. With this in mind, be alert and always keep on praying for all the saints."* ~ Ephesians 6:18 NIV

If we do not have a lifestyle of prayer, then we have no communication with God. If my husband and I go through a phase in our marriage where we are not communicating or are not emotionally intimate, as a woman I will feel disconnected. Even if we are having husband and wife relations in the bedroom. It is the same with our relationship with God. It is so important to keep constant communication with the Lord.

> *"To some who were confident of their own righteousness and looked down on everybody else, Jesus told this parable: "Two men went up to the temple to pray, one a Pharisee and the other a tax collector. The Pharisee stood up and prayed about himself: 'God, I thank you that I am not like other men—robbers, evildoers, adulterers—or even like this tax collector. I fast twice a week and give a tenth of all I get." "But the tax collector stood at a distance. He would not even look up to heaven, but beat his breast and said, 'God, have mercy on me, a sinner.' "I tell you that this man, rather than the other, went home justified before God. For everyone who exalts himself will be humbled, and he who humbles himself will be exalted."* ~ Luke 18:9- 14 NIV

Nothing proves to be more humbling than a devoted lifestyle of prayer. Prayer is often an unseen work and often marked by people who understand their need for their great, big, awesome God. Prayer is a spiritual posture, humbling ourselves before the Greatest One. Jesus left an amazing example of how to live submitted to a lifestyle of prayer. There are many illustrations in the Gospels of Him separating from the crowd to be alone. Having a lifestyle in which we have the self-discipline to remove ourselves from distractions for the purpose of prayer is one that reveals our maturation in the Lord, as well as the process of development in the things of the LORD. It is a type of passionate pursuit that needs to be constantly stirred to be sure the fire does not get quenched by the cares of this world.

What we do externally is never more important than the condition of our hearts, and our heart is always dealt with through a lifestyle of a devoted prayer life. Our dedication to prayer is the confirmation of our dependence on the LORD, and enables us to keep our hearts humble before Him. I can think of so many times in my life that I went to God to help me to learn how to pray. I didn't take classes to help me learn. The Holy Spirit is quick to teach us by how Jesus prayed.

When we conform to the lifestyle of Jesus and have a disciplined prayer life, by asking the Holy Spirit to teach us and we choose to yield to Him, He will teach us how to pray with His supernatural ability. The prayer life I speak of, is not one in which we bring a "to- do" list for the Lord. But, it is a process in which we allow God to pray His will, not our own, utilizing the Word of God and yielding to His Spirit, by being available to Him to live a life of prayer.

Why do prayers go seemingly unanswered? Many Christians are going through their journey of prayer by relying solely on human understanding and reasoning. We have been given the most precious gift. God Himself takes residence in those who trust and depend on the Lordship of Jesus Christ. No matter what branch of Christianity, we all have been adopted into the family by the same blood. This blood served as a ransom and a token of our inheritance to walk in covenant with

God and receive spiritual gifts. The spiritual gifts aren't for the sole purpose of displaying, but to be utilized by the BODY of Christ. Much of the Body is walking without the weaponry from God, naked without preparation and power. For it is only through HIS power that we have obtained power.

> *"For though we live in the world, we do not wage war as the world does. The weapons we fight with are not the weapons of the world. On the contrary, they have divine power to demolish strongholds. We demolish arguments and every pretension that sets itself up against the knowledge of God, and we take captive every thought to make it obedient to Christ."* ~ 2 Corinthians 10:3-5 NIV

> *"In the same way, the Spirit helps us in our weakness. We do not know what we ought to pray for, but the Spirit himself intercedes for us through wordless groans. And he who searches our hearts knows the mind of the Spirit, because the Spirit intercedes for God's people in accordance with the will of God."* ~ Romans 8:26-27 NIV

The most effective way of praying is described by Paul in 1 Corinthians 14:14-15 (NIV) *"For if I pray in a tongue, my spirit prays, but my mind is unfruitful. So what shall I do? I will pray with my spirit, but I will also pray with my understanding; I will sing with my spirit, but I will also sing with my understanding."*

Since we are a triune being, spirit, soul, and body, we must pray with an ability to affect each part. We must pray with understanding, in order to affect our soul (our mind, will, and emotions). However, we must build up our spirit man by charging our spirit with the Holy Spirit so that we can walk Spirit led. Without building up our spirit, we will be dominated by the flesh. When we are dominated by the flesh, it leads to destructive patterns that do not produce the abundant life Jesus has paid for us to have. In addition, allowing ourselves to be led by the flesh produces consequences in our lives that are painful and unnecessary.

God's main objective has always been and remained the same - to free His people from slavery by bringing them to the full understanding of Him as the Father that shares His love with His people whom He wants to adopt as His own. Through a strong prayer life, which submits our spirit, soul, and body, we can allow God to reverse any thought life, pain, or situation, causing us to no longer be identified with anything but freedom through Jesus Christ.

I have found some of the most powerful prayer circles were with people who allowed God to lead them both in the Spirit and in praying by declaring and decreeing the Word of God. The evidence of a powerful prayer life is the fruit in one's life. When we humble ourselves and begin declaring the Word into the atmosphere, we can be certain the Word will not return back void (Isaiah 55:11). As you open the Word and personalize it for your needs, and take ownership of the Word, you will be brought closer to the LORD and watch victory unfold for you.

An example of personalizing the Word is, when I was having emotional issues, I would search for scriptures that pertained to my circumstances and declare, Psalm 103:1 (NIV) *"Praise the Lord, my soul; all my inmost being, praise his holy name."* Since our soul is our mind, will, and emotions, I would declare out of my mouth, *"Monica, you will trust in the Lord and bless the Lord with all of your heart, all of your soul, ALL of your mind, and all of your emotions."* As I submit myself to the leading of the Holy Spirit, He prays His perfect will and peace floods me.

We cannot have an effective and powerful prayer life without getting baptized in the Holy Spirit, with the evidence of receiving the ability to pray in an unknown language. It makes perfect sense that in order to receive supernatural and spiritual breakthrough, we must submit to His Supernatural and Spiritual ability by the power of the Holy Spirit.

In order to produce spiritual breakthrough, we must allow the Holy Spirit to birth it. Which means yielding to His authority and not depending on our limited human efforts or abilities.

The greatest two life changing occurrences in my life has been, first, giving my life to the Lord Jesus Christ, and secondly, getting baptized in the Holy Spirit with the ability to speak in unknown languages. There are many times we don't know what to pray for. For many years, I didn't know how to submit to God, or how to pray specifically for His will. This affected every part of my life and stalled my healing. I was in a church service when the preacher explained the purpose of speaking in tongues. I wondered why anyone would want to pray like that. It seemed so strange and unusual and a bit too radical. But, he said something very profound that caught my attention and piqued my interest. He said, the enemy did not understand this language because it was from God and understood by Him only.

Since every gift, including salvation and speaking in tongues is received by faith, I didn't initially have the faith that the gift of speaking in tongues was really from God, nor that it was available for me. After about 6 months of searching the Word and asking God for more revelation, the Lord graciously gave me enough faith to receive it. Since the enemy had destructively interrupted my life too many times, I wanted every spiritual gift God wanted to give me. God is always awaiting our "YES!" Even if this is stretching you a bit, if you just agree to be open for the LORD to teach you, mature and equip you, and reveal the truth to you, HE will.

I felt peace flood me when I received this gift. But, after a while, I wasn't quite convinced praying with this new gift was changing my life. Other than feeling more peaceful, I had not really noticed anything dramatic after receiving my new prayer language, but by faith I continued. Then, one night I went to my oldest daughter's room after she was asleep. It is customary for me to check on the children before

I turn into bed. I put my hand on her forehead and began to pray in English. I felt a desire to pray in tongues and as I did, a deep burden and sadness came over me. I could've prayed scripture over her, but I did not understand the reason for my deep grief. I began to cry from a grief that came from deep within my belly. I had no reason to cry in the natural realm, but from within me, I was very burdened. I was taught from our pastor at the time to pray through until peace came, so I continued to pray in tongues until then.

The following day, she had music lessons. She took them in a private setting in a residential neighborhood. As her lesson finished, I was in a hurry to leave to do the next thing on my list. My daughter had forgotten her music folder inside and ran to go get it while I went to the vehicle. I told her I would wait alongside the curb. As I waited for her, I heard the sound of a diesel engine pressing impatiently on the gas. I looked in my rear view mirror and saw the face of an angry man who I had blocked from getting through. The residential street was narrow, so I backed up and moved over as much as I could so that he could get through. He wasn't happy with me, as he stepped on the pedal of his gas and revved it in order to express his anger and sped by.

Simultaneously, I saw a yellow folder, waving in the air, from my young daughter who could not see him through the vehicles that were parked alongside the curb. It seemed to play like a movie right in front of me. I saw him get angry, and speed by furiously. Then, I saw my daughter step out onto the street. I screamed out "Oh GOD!" At that very second, God reminded me of the night before. I saw myself praying for her, not knowing what I was praying about. As I'm seeing this in my heart, I see my daughter taking steps backwards, being saved from the truck by God. Never again have I questioned the power of yielding to the Holy Spirit. Since then, I have seen countless and mysterious resolutions of breakthroughs because of praying in tongues, not only in my life, but in the life of many.

Any believer can receive this gift. It only requires you desiring it. If you aren't there, and it seems too far-fetched, don't worry. God can even use this as a seed for the beginning of understanding. Every spiritual gift is awaiting you to ask God for the grace to have the faith to receive the gift. My job is just to share my testimonies and allow God to do the rest.

God's Word says we can come boldly to the throne of grace, with thanksgiving and praise. Therefore, you can ask Him anything. But, you must come with THANKSGIVING AND PRAISE and with the faith that He will bring your requests to pass. With your motives and heart pure before the Lord, He is prepared to bless you with every good thing. In my life, on a regular basis, I like to tell God what I am thankful for, and praise Him for it, and then make my petitions known. I like to imagine what the throne room of grace looks like. I imagine these big double doors with an ornate knocker and I knock (seek and you will find me, if you knock I will answer Matthew 7:7). When the door opens, I imagine Jesus opening the door for me. I can imagine lots of brilliancy and lots of white.

I imagine Him saying something like, "We have been waiting for you", as He leads me to the throne of the Father. In my experiences, Father God has a shape, but no way of defining Him. As I go there, I enjoy His presence which always brings me peace, and this is where I can bring my petitions for others, myself, or to just simply enjoy His wonderful and glorious presence. Without a strong prayer life, we cannot be strong Daughters of the KING. He is the source of life! In order to have more life, we do anything it takes to remove anything that prevents us from containing more of Him.

When I first gave my life to Jesus Christ, I did not know how to control myself. I had a great time living life as before, but I lived life not knowing I was separated from God. When I received the seed of salvation, I needed to be developed, like the process of transformation of a butterfly. However, we need to keep in mind there is a strategic assignment originating from the rebellious one, satan, to keep us from our fullest potential and to keep us from our purpose. God needs us to stay attached to His vine for adequate supply. So, that in our life, good fruit is developed as a confirmation to whom our nutrition comes from. When we stay on the Vine, we can have the nutrition, vitamins, and support we need in order to grow good fruit, so that we can be well developed. Abiding in prayer helps us to abide on the vine.

If you have prayed the same prayer over and over again without an outcome from God, trust His timings are perfect. When He speaks a promise, it is a done matter. Many times, we want the season to change, but there are things we need to gather in the season that we are in so we can utilize those things in the next season. There are things we need to acquire before we move forward. You are learning, growing, and increasing.

Pray with trust and expectancy that God is on your side and He shall complete what He begins. If you are not prepared for the next season, you won't be able to walk through it well. When you can trust His ways are higher, you are actually humbling yourself before His greatness. The greatest part of prayer is the intimacy that is developed between you and God.

There is a time to war in prayer and there is a time to just fellowship. Some of my most intimate times with God is when I just relish His presence. My prayer life didn't just grow from one night to another. It was a process; just like any friendship.

Although I spend time in prayer, most of my time with God is spent telling Him how awesome He is. Most of my prayer time is magnifying His power by exalting His name. The more we confess with our lips that He is great, the more His greatness is manifested in our lives. Our prayer time becomes more effective when our mind is focused on how great He is. At times in my Christian walk, I was told by leaders in the church that I needed to pray for 3-4 hours a day to be effective. After a while, praying showed up on my list of chores. Just like any other chore, it became something *I had* to do instead of something *I wanted* to do.

No person has the right to tell you how long you should pray. Prayer is not supposed to be like another chore. An active prayer life is keeping a strong friendship with God. When we have a strong friendship with God, we walk in great favor. When our prayer life is strong and others hurt us, just watch God deal quickly with the situation. Those that honor Him, He honors. Enjoying a relationship with God will touch every area in your life. An effective prayer life will bring an intimate relationship.

Prayer is a spiritual posture. Genuine prayer involves humbling ourselves and a changing of direction to the direction God is calling. Humble means to change our mind. It's submitting our mind, will, and emotions on what the Lord judges to be correct. You may believe you know the best resolution for what you are praying about. However, without getting God's aerial view on the situation, you are only spinning your wheels. We need to come into alignment with what God wants to happen in the situation. Humbling ourselves calls for us "to get over ourselves" and go to God and say, "I'm done, I don't have another way of solving this. I'm tired of all the ways I've tried solving it, so LORD, I'm done. What would you like? Change my heart. It is yours."

After we have learned His ways are better and less painful, we submit to His leading and His will much quicker than before. If you can pray with true humility, God Will HEAR your prayer and bring healing to every situation. Your prayer life will be accelerated, without any restraints whatsoever, and you will have so much more energy because you won't be weary. There's such great faith that comes with the confidence that you are heard by God who is Love, kind, merciful, long-suffering, most powerful, slow to anger, and the list goes on. He is forever wonderful.

Let's declare: *"I must humble myself and have a lifestyle of prayer and as a response, I will see great things happen in my life and in the lives of those I pray for."*

Remember to say the prayer out loud so that you can hear what you are praying.

Father, open my eyes to the things that are bringing distraction to my prayer life. Holy Spirit, I want You to pray through my lips. Jesus I want to be baptized in the Great Holy Spirit. I yield to You, knowing I am so limited and need You in every part of My life. I want to commit and surrender my ways, my gifts, and my life, under Your authority. Increase in me the desire for a more intimate prayer life, trusting You are available and desire me to come closer. Help me surrender and depend wholeheartedly on You. Renew my old ways and my old way of thinking. Search my heart and my ways, and teach me how to respond like Jesus. Help me to have self-discipline so that I can be separated for Your work as I yield my mouth to You, praying Your perfect and good will. Saturate me, Spirit of the living God, have Your way in my life as You bring me deeper into the understanding of how great it is to fellowship with You and abide in Your presence. Teach me how to pray, expect victory, and align my words with Yours. In Jesus name, Amen.

— Chapter 8 —

O-Obedience

L iving a life of Obedience—what does that look like? Being set free from a slavery mentality and an orphan spirit will help you stop striving in your life. Living a life of prayer and obedience will keep your ears inclined to the Lord, so that you become His instrument, changing the course for your family and all those that concern you.

> *"For if you live according to the sinful nature, you will die; but if by the Spirit you put to death the misdeeds of the body, you will live, **BECAUSE THOSE WHO ARE LED BY GOD** are sons of God."* ~ Romans 8:13 NIV

Let's declare: "I am a daughter of the Most High, therefore, I am led by God in all my ways."

God will always lead you to life, and provision is found where He leads. The Israelites followed the glory cloud and everywhere the glory cloud went, provision went, too. **The promise found in Romans 8:13 gives you and me a responsibility.** If we live for ourselves, we die spiritually and have oppression and no freedom. Or, it can be explained this way, if we choose to deny the Word of the Lord in our lives, we open the door to death onto our circumstances. However, **IF** we put our desires aside, and live according to His desires, this confirms our position as His children and leads us to life. *I believe the biggest idol of today is "self". I believe that is why one of the names of the Lord is "I AM". Meaning, not me, not you, but HE, The Great I AM.*

People in the world and in our churches should be able to see that you and I are legitimate children of the Most High by how we live our lives.

Obedience cannot come from a slavery mentality, because it becomes a religious activity that holds no value because it is done through a work based attitude. Obedience unto the Lord needs to come through honor. If we honor the Lord and trust Him with all of our hearts, we will be able to trust that what He asks of us is possible, and He is available to help us fulfill what He asks.

Since we should be in a constant process of maturation, we must realize if we are not in a process of transformation, we really aren't in a process towards conforming to His image. There are habits and thoughts God is calling for us to allow Him to change by bringing us closer to Him. It isn't because He wants to control us, it is because He sees their destructive consequences and loves us too much not to lead us to a place of safety. Just like a child does not have the wisdom or experience to know what is dangerous, a parent is to teach and protect their child by instructing them in the ways they should go. A compliant child will learn easier and have less destructive consequences than a child who is rebellious.

What is the habit that you would like God to help you overcome? Now, most of us would read through this part and not think we have a habit we need to stop. This is simply not the truth. All of us are in the process of some form of transformation. It could be yelling at your children to get their attention. It could be arguing with others in order to have the last word and to prove our point. It could be running late or not fulfilling your commitments, or picking up fast food on a regular basis when we should desire to live healthier.

We all have areas we have not allowed God to bring us out of. The point here is not to make anyone feel pointed out, but it is simply to point out something crucial. Where there are places within us that we are not experiencing the power of His Light, there are opportunities for us to be developed and reflect His resurrecting power, causing us to walk in deeper dimensions of freedom. These dimensions of freedom will cause satan to lose his footing in our lives.

As long as we live here on this earth, we will continue to be in a process towards the ultimate freedom. However, we do not want to stay in the process over the same detail. We want to continue to grow upwards. Every time you submit to God and His ways, by first, seeking Him to help you, to give you the grace to not succumb to your natural ways, and to respond the way His Word says you should, your habit will become one step closer to dying. If your habit is alive, as long as you nurture it, it's desire will continue to grow. BUT, if you allow it to starve, then it will become weak and begin to die.

As you abide on the vine, the nutrition from the Word of God will give you adequate supply to thwart off temptations, if you allow it to. This has to be done on a continuous basis. If you do not feed your Spirit, you will be weak, and it will be very difficult for you to see the strategies that satan has planned to keep you from developing in the Word. If you focus on strengthening your spirit with good spiritual food, the Word, prayer, and His presence, you will become strong. But, this also has to be done on a continuous basis. No athlete would remain strong if they discontinued their strength training exercises or their disciplined eating lifestyle. Whatever you feed your spirit, you will become. What we eat is revealed by the standard of our health. If we indulge in good things spiritually, it will be revealed in our responses.

When I was younger and lived in my parent's home, I would read in my room. I would read anything I could that would take me away from my emotional distress. I would also write. I would write mostly poetry. However, one of my favorite things to read were Harlequin Romance novels. Since I had an issue with lust, I found the romance novels were filled with romance, sex, and fed the things inside of me that had begun growing. I then graduated to watching romance movies. Unfortunately, many "romance" movies are filled with sex and sexual innuendos.

When the Lord started to reveal to me the type of roots that needed to be uprooted, He started to reveal to me that these movies and any type of sexual stimulants were stumbling blocks in my life. These "tools" could be used as baits of satan to keep me in bondage to tormenting thoughts about men. In order to give these thoughts no breeding ground, I needed to see these devices as poison to my thought life, my marriage, and my life in general. When you are unhappy in a marriage, any type of fantasy that is played in your mind or in a form of entertainment is disastrous because it only feeds into the discontentment.

Since you are the best one to recognize your weak areas, and you know what has tried to weaken you in your past, please know you are the one who is responsible for keeping the gate locked. God will help you, but you must sincerely want His help. The enemy will come in many packages to try to continue to hurt you in the areas God has freed you. Do not compromise! You are worth living in a higher realm of freedom.

Ask God to help you discern the "tools" satan uses to try to keep you from growing. The bait on a hook doesn't seem like very much when the fish tries to take a bite. It's only when it's out of the water and striving to breathe with a hook in its mouth that it realizes, the bait used was so much more than it seemed. The fish only wanted a little bite, but it cost him his life. We need to be mindful we do not consume "baits" that will eventually take us out of safety. Be mindful of the movies and music that you listen to and make sure they are not trying to lure you in and push you further into a place of weakness.

Fear, is another very common device satan loves to keep us in. Watching fearful movies produces fear in many different ways, such as putting ideas in your head, hearing eerie sounds in the house, your children having nightmares, etc. Do not let satan cast bait in your pond. Believe me, he is casting. My prayer is that you would realize what he baits you with and when it is cast. This is not written to you to tell you all the do's and don'ts. I am simply addressing the consequences. When we stay under the protection of the Lord, satan cannot torment us with them because we haven't given him ground to do it. I finally got sick and tired of him tormenting my dreams, my marriage, my children, finances, etc., so I asked God to reveal to me where was I giving him access to hurt me.

Are you sick and tired too? Let's start closing the gates and ask God to lead us. Jesus came to give us LIFE MORE ABUNDANTLY (John 10:10). I am simply asking you to ask the Lord if the things you are attracted to are the things He thinks are good enough for you.

Thoughts:

_____

_____

_____

Increasing our level of obedience to Him, depends greatly on us knowing that God is not sitting in heaven with a gavel waiting for us to mess up. He simply loves us so much! He does not want us to suffer the consequences of undermining laws that are in place for our protection. Obedience out of adoration to Him, reveals you have experienced the grace and love of God.

As women, we do not have to say "yes" to everyone and everything. Sometimes our compassion and mercy prevents us from allowing God to step into situations. Often, we hear of someone that we have been praying for has run away from God and we want to run and save them. What if God wanted to use that situation to draw them closer to Him and soften their heart to call upon Him? Many times God wants exactly that, and after preparing their heart, He will send you or another laborer to minister to them. The preparation was so important because it positioned them to be able to receive it.

The enemy can keep us running around like a hamster on the wheel because we think we are doing "the good Christian thing". We belong to God, not every person. So, Stop!! Ask God in everything, "Is this my responsibility?" Are you calling me to do something here? What does that look like? When? How much? Before you commit to helping someone, be quick to make sure God is calling you to do it. Because if He is, grace will be there.

Was it easy for me to walk away from relationships that I cared about? No, not at all. However, was I worth it? You bet! ARE YOU WORTH receiving the protection of staying under the umbrella of the Word? Are you worth EVERY blessing? YOU BET YOU ARE!!!! It does not have anything to do with being easy, but it has everything to do with your value, your purpose, your potential, and fulfilling your God given dreams. Even more than that, where you pioneer the way, your children will not have to work as hard as you did. Why? Because you are paving the way.

You are their best and most efficient teacher. What you sow into the ground, they reap! You are leaving a legacy for them. That's exciting, but a huge responsibility! I am so grateful that my children never have to go through the things I went through. I am grateful from here on out, our lineage only improves and strengthens. The more you encounter God and His love and walk away from things that aren't the best for you, the easier obedience will become because you understand TRUE love and the security it brings.

"If you are not disciplined—and everyone undergoes discipline— then you are not legitimate, not true sons and daughters at all." ~
Hebrews 12:8 NIV

This promise of discipline has a responsibility for all of us. If we live for ourselves, we will become spiritually weak, oppressed, and our freedom becomes limited. Spiritual oppression is terrible because it happens step by step. One step of disobedience at a time puts us back into a yoke of slavery.

> *"It is for freedom that Christ has set us free. Stand firm, then, and do not let yourselves be burdened again by a yoke of slavery."*~ Galatians 5:1 NIV.

If we put our desires aside and live according to His desires, our submission reflects we are His children. Isn't it amazing, that an obedient child could be mixed with a large group of children, and once they hear their parents calling for them, they recognize their voice in the sea of voices and run to their parent? Let us be the obedient child who is quick to respond to the voice of our Father.

> *"Trust in the Lord and do good; dwell in the land and enjoy safe pasture. Take delight in the Lord, and he will give you the desires of your heart. Commit your way to the Lord; trust in him and he will do this."* ~ Psalm 37: 3-5 NIV

> *"... Do you think all God wants are sacrifices—empty rituals just for show? He wants you to listen to him! Plain listening is the thing, not staging a lavish religious production. Not doing what God tells you is far worse than fooling around in the occult. Getting self-important around God is far worse than making deals with your dead ancestors. Because you said "no" to God's command, He says "no" to your kingship."* ~ 1 Samuel 15:22-23 MSG*

Not obeying God is worse to Him than witchcraft! Just do what you feel God is leading you to do. Don't go through life with a mindset of "Oh my goodness, I have to change everything!" Do not live life by a checklist of worries about where you failed. Just listen to your God! He will walk you through the journey of obedience. He will lead you *through* the journey. If we make it about ourselves, or what we can offer God, it makes us responsible for our own change, which gives us a sense of self- importance. Without God doing the work, it will become mundane activity, and will bring bondage and not change. Come to God with a yielded heart, prepared to partner with Him through a life of adventure.

In Matthew 8:5-13, the centurion had great faith because he understood authority. Jesus told him he had not met another person with such great faith. Notice how Jesus didn't even say that to one of his disciples who saw His power manifested on a regular basis. Understanding His authority will be the activation to our faith. When we understand wholeheartedly the Kingship of Jesus and your position of being under Jesus, then you will have authority because of His Kingship. What is so amazing is that no matter what opposition or demon of hell comes your way, as long as you are submitted to the authority of Jesus Christ, no weapon can prosper.

Kingship is a position, an office or dignity of a king. Our position, of being a daughter of the KING of kings, has granted us a position of authority. Our authority is wrapped in our obedience and anointing. When we are walking in obedience, submitted to God, we are automatically walking in His anointing that breaks EVERY yoke. In today's culture, in the western church, we do not really understand yoke. Although I am from Texas, I have never had to yoke two animals together. I am a city girl! What the Holy Spirit showed me through an illustration of a pair of ox, is when the farmers plow the field using two oxen, a yoke is put on the pair so that their united strength will pull with greater force. However, if one of the oxen is moving at a different speed than the other, there will be an imbalance.

I had a Catholic wedding, and one of the traditional symbols is to incorporate the use of a lasso during the ceremony. My grandmother crocheted a beautiful wedding lasso for us. The lasso has two loops and as the couple is kneeling down, one side is to be looped over the groom and the other over the bride, as a symbol of a Holy Covenant of the two journeying through life together. Using this illustration of the lasso, we are called to walk with God in covenant.

The Word says the anointing breaks the yoke. Every yoke, which is what tries to oppose you and keep you from going forward in life, the anointing of God breaks it so that you can walk in your destiny. It is important that we do not allow just any person to be in our yoke. It's quite frustrating to be paired with those who do not want to walk with you where God has called you. Not everyone is called to be in your "yoke". When you are in a yoke with Jesus Christ, you can walk uninhibited (Matthew 11:28-30)!

The soul ties I mentioned in chapter 1 are very much like yokes (a device that joins two together). Soul ties prevent us from walking in freedom and are attached to circumstances and people. Rape, past sexual relationships, and even relationships and friendships with people I loved and honored, who eventually brought me pain, were causing a tie to my soul that kept me in bondage because my soul was still responding to the familiarity of the pain. Let us no longer have destructive ties to our soul. If you have not broken ties in your soul realm from situations and past relationships, now is the time to do so. I am going to lead you in a prayer and by faith I need you to imagine a "life line" being cut. When you cut these ties, you will be able to move forward.

Remember to say the prayer out loud so that you can hear what you are praying.

Father, reveal to me any ties You want to be cut in my life. Reveal to me the names and situations that are still acting as a "life-line" so that I can operate in freedom. I do not want these destructive ties to my soul anymore. In the name of Jesus and by faith, I cut the ties off my soul from _____ (say every person's name out loud) I do not want to be tied to these people or these circumstances _____ (name each circumstance). I apply the blood of Jesus, which brings resurrection to my soul, and speak life over me in Jesus name. I renounce all works of satan over my life and declare I am a daughter of the KING who has been ransomed by His blood. By the grace of God, I shall walk in every spiritual inheritance.

When we know the character of God, we can trust our Father with our own experiences and obedience becomes second nature. When we really trust that He truly cares about our joy, our peace, our present, past, and future. That He is for us, in the big things and in the little things, it's easy to trust and obey Him. We will realize obedience brings blessing and protection. There is no other person that is more for you than the One who created you. No other person wants us walking in complete freedom, which is why He wants to remove us from situations that keep us bound. Many times it is very difficult to listen, much less obey what God wants because we do not trust Him. There have been times in my life when I saw God as someone with a whip behind my back, or someone who wanted to dictate my life. This could not be further from the truth. All He wants to do is to keep us in freedom.

It is only when we have not been perfected in knowing who He is that we feel we are sacrificing. When Abraham put Isaac on the altar (Genesis 22), he had already established a relationship with God before God asked him for Isaac. Since he had already established God was good, he was able to trust that God had a way out. God will never ask you for a sacrifice He hasn't already made a way for you to give.

Because Abraham trusted in God, he was able to give him his son. God not only saved his son, but also blessed him more than he could have ever given to God.

You can never out give Him. It is the relationship that you build with God now that will determine the confidence in Him later. He will never ask more of us than the grace He has already given us in order to complete the transaction of obedience for blessings and more intimacy. He will lead us to the journey, through the journey, and beyond the journey, to allow us to develop more trust in Him, giving us testimonies to share with others.

A runner would never run a long race without the proper preparation to complete it or without developing in endurance and strength. The time to train is NOW! God will develop you before He sends you to more difficult assignments. As you move forward in your journey, He will give you what you need in the measure you need it. Write down the words God gives you personally that He is calling you to fulfill, and trust He will give you the direction and provision as you need it and when you need it, step by step.

Using the illustration of the development process of the butterfly and spiritual growth, stay in the atmosphere in which you can thrive and grow into a deeper dimension of intimacy with the LORD. Stay hungry! What would happen to that caterpillar if it stopped eating, or didn't eat enough? Would he become a butterfly if he did not get the proper nourishment by eating continuously? The acronym P.O.W.W.E.R., will help us stay on target, like the hungry caterpillar. If we feel we aren't experiencing an intimate relationship with our Daddy God, then we need to see if we are putting that acronym to work in our lives.

In November 2008, as I was growing in my prayer life and learning to listen for His voice, I discerned that I heard God ASK me to have another baby. This was definitely not something I or my husband wanted to hear. I was not ready to do what God had called me to do concerning this. With my pregnancies, I got sick and had long, excruciating labors and we thought we were completely done with having babies. However, I discerned God tell me that we had never asked Him how many children we should have. Well, it never dawned on us to do that. I felt God say— "Your two children were your idea" — (they were both planned and it took about a year to conceive each) — But, this child would be born out of faith and obedience." So I cried, and asked God to forgive us for not asking Him how many children He had called us to raise. I told the Lord that if this plan was really from Him, He would have to supernaturally change our hearts and that the IUD inside of me would have to be released by Him--- that would be a sign to us.

After I told my husband, I thought he would embrace the idea right away. I was wrong---it took a long time of praying in the Spirit (in tongues) to change our hearts and for me to realize that I was wrong to pray that God would have to supernaturally remove the IUD. I was wrong because I wanted God to do all of the work and God required me to believe Him, trust Him, and I needed to be obedient to what He had asked of us. My husband was finally at a place of being on board with this idea, and I scheduled the appointment to have the IUD removed. We decided not to "try" to conceive, but to allow God to do what He wanted to do. Our hearts were ready and prepared to welcome another child.

In January 2010, (2 years after I heard from the Lord) we went on a weekend getaway and while there, I had a dream. I dreamed I was giving someone a tour of our home and one of the bedrooms was a nursery, decorated for a girl. The person I gave a tour to asked me if I was pregnant. I told her no, but we were waiting. When I woke up I realized my breasts were very tender and I was supposed to start my menstrual cycle during the trip and had not.

On the way home from our trip, I decided to get a pregnancy test. I was so excited that I took it right away, and sure enough, I was pregnant. After finding out I was pregnant, it was confusing as to why I wasn't pregnant in the dream. Why had I prepared a nursery in the dream, without being pregnant? Later, I would find out why!

At our first sonogram, the doctor told us we had come in too early, therefore, the heartbeat could not be detected. We scheduled an appointment the following week, still thanking God for the gift of life He had entrusted to us.

At the second sonogram, the doctor seemed concerned and told us he could see a mass in my womb, but again no heartbeat could be detected. This time we were a bit concerned! We went home and charged forward with prayer. Declaring and decreeing this was a miracle to be used by God. During this time, I would go into one of our rooms in our house, and I would pray for hours. I would put my hands on my womb and declare life. I felt a measure of burden. Our children knew we were pregnant as well as all those we served at church. I was so convinced our prayers would be answered in the way of a healthy baby.

Every time I would go to the doctor, I was adamant a heartbeat would be found. On our third appointment, the doctor told me to prepare for a miscarriage and gave me a prescription for the pain. The doctor wanted us to go through the process at home, and be prepared for what was coming. Initially I was shocked. "Look again", I said. "There has to be a heartbeat." And still, no heartbeat was found.

As I walked into the elevator, as soon as the doors closed I said, "I am not going to put my faith there, God said to have a baby, and I said I would. My heart has changed. I want this baby. I expect this child to live." That night I had another dream. Our oldest daughter was taking a shower with a newborn baby boy. She held him up to the water where it poured out. In the dream, I stood near the shower with a very pregnant

Take Your Position Daughter

belly. When I awoke, I wondered to myself, how I could possibly be that far along in pregnancy and have a newborn baby.

I wasn't very happy with God. I didn't understand the dream and I was still adamant that He was going to breathe life into the life in my womb. I was very honest with the Lord in my anger. "I don't know how I feel about you Lord. I don't know why You would ask me to do something that would cause me such grief." I felt very separated from His love, wondering what I did wrong. How did I cause this? Was it something I did? Could I have done something better?

On that visit, I was told by my doctor to go to the hospital to make sure I didn't need surgery. I was angry. I was angry with God and for the first time in years, I didn't want to pray. I didn't want to read scripture, which had been my lifeline for years at this point. Sitting in a hospital gown, being prepared for an examination, and again, no heartbeat being found, I felt abandoned by this great God I thought I knew.

It was around 10:00 pm when a knock came and it was a pastor from our church at the time. My husband went out into the hall to see who was knocking and came to tell me Pastor Dwayne Deason had arrived to check on me. I whispered, "I don't want to see him." But, as soon as I whispered that, he walked right into the room. Pastor Deason was an instrument sent by God, and He used his coming to see me to remind me I was not forgotten.

The first thing he said was, "I didn't come to pray, or to talk, I just came by to give you a hug and let you know we love you." It was just what I needed! Sometimes what we need is not given by the people we think it should come from, and at that moment I needed a Daddy's hug. I needed unreligious actions. Sometimes in the midst of a trial, that's all God wants to tell you, "I love you, I want you, and I want to hug you."

A week went by, and there was still no progress. We were still praying and believing for a miracle. One day in my prayer room, I began to say,

"I speak life over you baby, in Jesus name. I command your heart to beat. I command tissues to line up." At that moment of great faith and expectancy, the atmosphere shifted. I could sense the presence of Jesus, and the Holy Spirit, which are two distinct presences. Suddenly, as tears flowed, I saw the feet of Jesus, right before my eyes. I saw my tears flood over His feet and even in my great distress, I saw me wipe them with my hair. In the midst of my grief, deep within my core, I knew that even in that moment, He was worthy to be praised.

My worship ushered the Holy Spirit to bring the dream to my remembrance. The one of my oldest daughter holding a newborn baby boy up to the water in a shower. I heard Him say in my heart, "This child will never know sin." I thought about that statement and tried to process it. "This child will never know sin." "How could someone not know sin?", I thought. In order not to know sin, he must never walk on this earth. "Lord," I said, "You are the God of miracles, and I can't agree with death." I heard Him say, "Your faith pleases me. This child will never know death, nor know sin. He will teach you things when you arrive."

At that moment, I sensed angels come into the room, and I don't know how this works, but this is what I saw. I saw a room in Heaven, like a nursery and it had many jars of all sizes, from small, medium, and large. In these jars were babies of different sizes. On earth we call them fetus', but, in Heaven they are all babies. These babies stayed in the jar until they were mature enough to come out. Then, I saw an angel on a rocking chair and this angel rocked and rocked and was nursing our son. Jeremiah was the name we gave him. I wept loudly to the Lord, "It isn't fair Lord, I wanted to nurse my son." He said, "My ways are higher. But I need you to know, I am STILL the God of the impossible. I AM still the God of restoration. I AM still the God that fulfills My promises." With a quick flash, I saw a young boy about 5 or 6 years old, running in a field, laughing, as if playing tag. He had dark hair and wore white. I just knew that was our son.

A week passed and I had another doctor's appointment, and still no heartbeat. On that evening, I went to bible school. It was a Tuesday and I sat next to the most compassionate and sweetest lady I have ever met to this day. I could feel my body responding to a miscarriage with cramping. During the teaching, I began to weep. I am sure she was wondering why I was weeping, and finally I whispered to her. She put her arms around me, which is what I needed that night, the love of a mother. When I went home that night, I took half of my prescribed pain reliever because I am quite sensitive to medication.

We have always taught our children that our God was and is good. And despite the fact that we live in an imperfect world, He remains good. My daughter was with me in the shower when the room began to spin. I sat down on the seat of the shower. As I sat, I heard my daughter yelling out for my husband, but I couldn't respond. I could feel matter being released out of my body and down my legs, but I couldn't do anything about it. I was numb. The medication had caused me to be unable to react. My husband came in and all I wanted to do was protect my young daughter from seeing anything traumatic like seeing her mother bleed. But, I couldn't say anything, and my husband was only thinking of me. As mothers, we don't want our children to hurt, we prefer to do the hurting.

As I hear her screaming and could not protect her, I hear my husband calling out for trash bags. I hear my young son coming with trash bags and I want to yell out, "Don't come in here. Stay downstairs", but it's too late. My daughter and son were trying to clean things up while my husband had me on the toilet. Here I was believing God for a miracle, and we were having this traumatic event happen in our home. Why didn't they perform surgery? Why did my children have to go through this? What was all this for? So, now, not only am I praying for the healing of our family towards the loss of Jeremiah, but now am praying against trauma for our children and what they saw.

After the process was over, the Holy Spirit came to fill the positions that people failed to fill in my life. When I was severely depressed, I didn't want to hear from anyone. Not even my husband at times. Women attach to their babies in the womb. Men are usually more visual and tend to attach more when the baby arrives, at least in my experience. It wasn't that my husband didn't mourn, he just mourned differently. I didn't want to talk about it. I just wanted to be alone. The day after I miscarried, I asked a friend to care for our children. My husband was prepared to take off, but I wanted to be alone. That day, I lay in my bed, and I wailed before the Lord. Crying out, at the top of my voice, "WHY????" I was still upset and angry and I felt abandoned in my faith. I could sense demonic oppression in the room, laughing at me and my faith. I didn't have the strength to fight. I didn't care to fight back. But God, in His awesomeness!

At that moment, in my time of great despair, I saw myself in this dark pit, like a small cave, sitting in a fetal position, rocking back and forth. I didn't want to look up or anywhere at all. I just wanted to keep my head buried under my arms. I was spiritually, emotionally, and physically wounded. As I rocked back and forth, God expanded my vision, and right beside me still in the fetal position, I saw Jesus Christ sitting there with me. He waited, and all of a sudden, He got up. He extended His arms out to me, as if to say, "Okay, that's enough. It's time to get up." He gave me His hand and said, "It's time to rise."

After that encounter with God, it gave me the strength to believe in the impossible even in the midst of impossibilities. I have learned in my experiences that Jesus Christ goes through the pain with us, but loves us too much to keep us there.

One day while I was in my room praying and worshipping, the Lord took me to Heaven. I had a quick glimpse of a little boy once, prior to this incident, but I had been curious and asked God for confirmation. In my time of being in Heaven, whether in the body or not, I do not know, I saw myself in a boat and mountains were just up ahead. While on a river, I saw the snow topped mountains with brilliant Light on the other side of the mountain. I wanted to get to that brilliance as soon as I could because I knew that's where Jesus was. I got into the boat and there were two oars. The oars had names written on them, "Praise" and "Prayer". As I used those oars, "Praise" and "Prayer", the faster I went up the river toward the mountain with the brilliant light where the Glory was. Suddenly, the water ran out and I stepped outside of the boat. Although the water was very shallow, when I stepped out, my feet didn't get wet.

As I stepped out, I could smell the presence of what smelled like a garden, one I've never smelled on earth. The smell permeated my nostrils and as I smelled it, I could also taste it. I've never eaten flowers on earth, not any kind at all, but I knew these were flowers which I had no memory of coming in contact with before. I learned during this encounter that whatever you think, the response comes automatically. I thought to myself, "Where am I?" And suddenly, I knew I was in Heaven, in a field. I thought to myself, why does this field look familiar, and instantly I knew. I remembered that this was the field I had seen Jeremiah running in in one of my previous visions. As soon as I remembered the field, I thought, "I wonder where Jer..." The moment I thought it, I saw him hugging my neck, nuzzling his face into my neck as if he recognized my smell, like all children know their mothers smell. It was so very beautiful. Thinking about it even now, tears flow from my soul.

Experiencing hugging someone I had so wanted to meet while on this earth was a supernatural occurrence that I had never planned. What a gift! But when I left this vision, I wept and wept when I realized I was no longer there, but not because of Jeremiah. As a matter of fact, I had forgotten earthly realms such as my role of being a wife and a mother to our other two children while I was there. Because of the peace I received in Heaven, I didn't want to come back. I was so wrapped in the presence of God's Kingdom and His glory, I could still smell the aroma of Heaven on me and my clothes when I returned. I cried and said, "Lord, I don't want this to end. I don't want to be separated from Your Glory and Your home." It was so difficult experiencing such a small amount of Heaven and it being the best thing that has happened in my life and then having to leave. What a joy we have coming, for all eternity, for those that choose to live and serve the Lord Jesus!

The Holy Spirit took me on a journey, and I asked Him to help me help my children heal from our loss. I didn't have the energy to study how to heal after a miscarriage or ask others. It has been my experience that if we ask Him, He will lead. It is the same truth for anyone. He gave me the idea to buy a pretty box. We all wrote letters and drew pictures to put in this box, along with the sonogram pictures. This brought much closure and healing to our children. In my life, I have had very few mentors and teachers. It has been only the Holy Spirit who has filled those positions. When I pushed people away because of my grief, it was the great Comforter who came. He is enough!

It was a painful time. Many times, I would remind God of our conversation, of Him asking me to conceive out of my obedience to Him. In my childlike faith—I expected this was going to be an amazing testimony—proving to everyone that God does amazing miracles. He does, but it didn't turn out the way I thought. Many times when we are obedient to God, it seems we have it all figured out— but we are basing it on our own human standards. The nights that led up to my miscarriage were filled with times of desperation to the Lord. One thing I focused on is that I would praise Him despite what He allowed me to go through. I worshipped Him until the tears ran out, and all I did was sit at His feet. I know God did not cause the miscarriage.

"For the LORD is good and His love endures forever; His faithfulness continues through all generations." ~ Psalms 100:5 NIV

127

During this time, I saw the Lord on several occasions. I wouldn't trade this part of my journey, because I learned lessons that I would never have learned had I not gone through this time of loving Him despite the outcome. I still believe God was and is pleased with my faith.

Three months after I miscarried, I got pregnant with our youngest. Since it took one year to conceive each of the other two children in my late twenties, it was supernatural for us to become pregnant in that very short time at thirty-eight years old. During the three months of prior to me getting pregnant, we prepared our home in obedience to Go for our baby, just like the dream I had. She has been everything God has promised her to be. She has been such a blessing—and we call her "God's plan was best." Even the first night we brought her home, she slept through the night. I recall waking up at 6:00 am the next morning in a frenzy because I hadn't fed the baby. She is very vocal and will tell it like it is.

We named our son, who is now in Heaven, Jeremiah. He was my sacrifice of love and worship that God used in order for me to know Him as the God of Restoration. I do know that God uses that seed to bring forth a harvest. Not only was Jeremiah a seed for me---but he is the seed God uses for all those that I teach about restoration and that we can love Him in all circumstances. Although I do not understand it all, I know Jeremiah is doing something amazing in Heaven and still being used for great purposes in the Kingdom of God. With obedience comes blessings---and the blessings are immeasurable. A seed of obedience takes time to harvest---depending on the size of the harvest.

If you have had a miscarriage, abortion, a baby or a child that is no longer here, know that they are in Heaven. There is still a purpose and a plan for their lives, an eternal life that cannot be ended. Life continues in Heaven, life without obstacles, pain, or death. When you arrive in Heaven, they will teach you and will be waiting for you. They will know more about our eternal home than we do and will be glad to be our tour guide. Babies that never step on earth can fulfill purposes we can never fill, because they never knew sin. Therefore, they are on a higher level in Heaven. When we leave this earth to be transformed into our eternal state to live in Heaven, our legacy on earth continues, as well as the rewards from God attached to those legacies. Our babies that live in Heaven continue to build a legacy through the words and love that remain within us. They can bring comfort to those that we can identify with because they too have been separated from their child.

God gave us many years to prepare our hearts in order to desire His plan. Because I knew the character of God, I could continue to praise Him, even when it was difficult. Our Father God uses the seed of Jeremiah in order to teach about restoration and the sacrifice of worship. Although God allowed us to go through a time of mourning, 6 days after I miscarried, I felt compelled to tell a lady I was working with that I had miscarried 6 days before, but I believe I saw him running in a field in Heaven. She began to weep and said eight years prior to our conversation she had lost her twins through miscarriage. God gave me the grace to minister His hope and love to her.

I have found that every story you have walked through in your life has hope and victory attached... even the sad ones. If you allow God to heal you from the stories that are painful, He will cause you to overcome with the ability to share the gift with someone who needs to hear it. After He has healed you, every single time you share your stories, you are allowing Him to reconcile people back to His heart. Don't let satan have the last word. Let God heal you where it hurts so that your stories can be turned around and used for GOOD.

Recognize that God is the perfect Father, who is good all of the time and there is no darkness in Him.

"God is light, in Him there is no darkness at all." ~ 1 John 1:5

As you grow in this revelation, it will become easier to trust Him and be obedient.

Jesus fulfilled His mission being entirely obedient, because He was so connected to the heart of the Father. He was so submitted to the Father because He knew Him and trusted in Him. When we have become submitted to the Father, it is because we have come to know and trust Him. What you are learning about the Lord in your process right now will be important to draw from in the next step of your journey, which takes us to our next letter---the First "W".

Remember to pray out loud so you can hear.

FATHER, prepare my heart for obedience to Your Word. Give me tangible experiences in which I can grow in obedience so that my life brings You glory. Help me surrender and submit myself to You, submitting myself to Your Kingship in every facet. Thank you for the grace as I step out with You, choosing You above all else. Help me draw boundaries with situations and people and only put my hand to the works You have called me to, learning how to withdraw from what you have not. Give me the courage to withdraw from atmospheres and people that are destructive to my growth in You. In Jesus name, Amen.

—Chapter 9—

W-Worship

Worship has been the main component of bringing me out of the darkness and into the Light of healing. When you catch the heart of worship and receive a spirit of worship, no matter what situation you are in, you will see victory. I have seen what worship has done in my life, and the lives of many. There have been times, that I have been in an unsafe area and I'm a bit concerned about my well-being. When I begin to worship quietly, it ushers the Kingdom of God and brings protection. Not only does God provide protection through worship, but the atmosphere changes when we release worship. God's favor resides with every worshipper.

Sitting in the car with my windows rolled down, waiting for my son to get out of his fitness class, a man was parked beside me. He was yelling at the person he was speaking to, cursing her and using derogatory names. I got upset about the words he was using towards this person. I prayed silently, "Lord, I don't want to hear this. Can you please quiet him, or calm him?" I also prayed for the person on the other end of the line. I whispered, "I Declare peace and joy", and I began to worship. "You are awesome and magnificent God, worthy to be praised." There was no way the man could have heard me, especially over his yelling. He turned on his car, and moved to another side of the parking lot. Worship changes atmospheres and makes the enemy and his devices run the opposite way! The presence of the Lord changes atmospheres when you open your mouth. Since the joy of the LORD is our strength, there are strategies against your joy from the enemy.

The level of our understanding will determine the demonstration of our worship. If we don't understand His deity and, His character, we won't be able to understand worship. How we worship displays our understanding of who He is. People will go to a sports game, paint their faces, and act like fools. Then, they will come into a worship service where the people love to worship the Lord, and say, "These people are weird, why do they raise their hands." They just don't understand and haven't encountered God in a deeper way.... yet. My prayer is that we would become radical worshippers who do not care what people think, because our love for God will outweigh the image we want to portray. The more you allow yourself to become lost in worship and His presence, the more the enemy wants to flee from you.

In the book of Ezekiel, lucifer was in charge of the worship. He actually had strings built in his chest. He knows how important worship is and because of that, he wants to keep you from the revelation of how important worship is for your freedom. Just like love and forgiveness looks like something, worship looks like something too.

Our lives should look different once we have the adoptive encounter with God. I was freed from much, therefore I love Him much. If it weren't for God, I would have a completely different life, still living as a slave to satan. You cannot express devotion through words, it is only expressed in action. If a sponge sits on the counter and never gets wet, it will not be used as it was intended. If we do not soak up His presence with worship and prayer in the privacy of our homes, we will never be able to pour out on others.

True worship is living a life before Him, abiding in His presence, allowing Him to lead us in all things. We must soak in His presence so that we can fill our sponge and pour Him on others. But, worship is not limited there, we must live a life of worship. Allow Him to be the Lord of everything, your actions, your words, in what you see, in what you hear, in all you do. Allowing God to have every part of you, your past, present, and future, to use for His glory, is what a life of worship is really all about. Living a life of worship is not just what we say, it is seen in what we do. When we recognize just how much Jesus Christ has done for us, we will love Him more.

> *"Therefore, I tell you, her many sins have been forgiven-as her great love has. Shown. But whoever has been forgiven little love little."* ~ Luke 7:47 NIV

Worship with your lifestyle *by living* a life of sacrificial worship and laying your life down. If we want to keep satan away, Jesus reiterates the first two of the ten commandments, in Matthew 4:10.

> *"Jesus said to him, 'Away from me, satan! For it is written: 'Worship the Lord your God, and serve him only.'"*

Jesus serves only the Father. His life was lived as one laid down for the desire of another, His Father. If we are to be like Jesus, we must also live a life laid down by serving Jesus. There are two parts of the instruction in Matthew 4:10. However, first, Jesus put satan in his place by telling him to depart....be gone...go away. Then he continued to quote the scriptures, *"For it is written, "Worship the Lord your God, and serve Him only."* Turning our backs on satan is evidenced by worshipping God and serving Him. First, we must worship (submit, adore, kneel down to worship), and secondly, we must serve (to render service) which is also another form of worship.

How do we worship? Is worshipping God only done with music and a loud voice? True worship is shown in how we live our lives. True worship is living a life before Him, abiding in His presence, allowing Him to lead us in all things. Abiding in Peace (JESUS) —even when we are being pulled to chaos.

We are made in God's likeness and image. We are given eyes to see the broken and wounded, arms to gather and bind the pain, hands to extend the love, gentleness and tenderness of God, feet to take us to the afflicted, and legs to support us so that we do not fall. WE ARE CALLED to look for the broken to share the love that is in Christ Jesus and impart the Kingdom. We are called to wipe their tears and reveal the character of God and bring resurrection to those that are dead spiritually, through the power of the Holy Spirit and in the name of Jesus.

Many times, Christians are such in a hurry to leave an atmosphere, whether it be their workplace or a gathering with family members who do not follow God. However, God is calling us to submit our mind, body, and will to Him, in worship, so that He can be represented in a place where no person is representing Him. You have assignments from God to be His extension. Don't be in such a hurry to leave a place without getting the strategy from God and His assignments for your life. When you have been faithful to where He has called you to serve Him, at the appointed time, which is determined by Him, He will promote you to another field.

Do not underestimate the power of your worship, which is a life laid down before the LORD in surrender. Recognize where "spiritual death" is operating. Recognize where, even believers, are responding from a place of death. And since you have received the impartation of resurrection in the areas of your past wounds, you can impart life onto those who need it. Love covers! When His presence is more real than our physical realm and we step into His presence, nothing else matters. It is our hiding place. A place where we are hidden and cannot be found by the enemy. Your imagination is a powerful tool. I like to imagine God right in front of me while I worship. As I connect my soul (my mind) to God and see Him with my eye of faith, His presence increases dramatically and takes me into further realms of His manifested presence, one that I can experience. There are times that I dance, or just lay in surrender, sing, clap, shout, or thump my hands, as if playing an instrument.

Worship always looks like something. If you can recognize your worship takes you to the place where the Glory (manifested presence of God) is, everything that does not belong to you, will begin to fall away when you are in that place. It doesn't matter if it is a physical ailment, like a headache, depression, or marital issues. If you can get to the place of true uninhibited worship, you will get to the place where freedom lies, and you become addicted and accustomed to going into the place of glory, which is found in magnifying His presence.

When my daughter was around eight years old, we had planned for her to have a party with her closest friends. We had been planning it for a few weeks, and the weekend we had scheduled was the only weekend available for quite some time. The day of the party she got sick, with a fever and cold like symptoms. I did not want to cancel the party. She had been looking forward to it, and I had done all the work it takes to have a party (moms you know what I mean)!

The wonderful news is, I had received the revelation of worship, and how worshipping God ushers in the anointing of the Lord. And where His presence is, there is freedom! I went to the bed where my daughter was asleep. I laid my hands on her and began to wholeheartedly praise God. I began to give God glory and honor by telling Him how awesome, magnificent, perfect, and just He is! After several hours of just worshipping and becoming more aware of His presence, she was healed! No fever, no runny nose, nothing, nada, zilch! She had her party and what a wonderful time we had! God cares about *all* that concerns us.

Now listen, if you have never done this before, this may feel strange to you. That's ok! I wasn't able to worship uninhibitedly overnight. However, the more you recognize His lavish love, and His desire to help you in all things, you will expect His goodness every single time. One of the best things to do to get yourself plugged into the atmosphere of worship is to sing a scripture. Since you can do this by yourself and are the only one that can hear yourself, it doesn't matter how you sound! It's the heart God cares about. When you allow yourself to sing to the Lord, it will give you much freedom! I greatly encourage you to do this.

As an exercise, let's sing unto the Lord, so that you can experience what I am wanting to impart to you. Remember, no other person is listening. If you don't want to hear yourself, put some instrumental music on to drown out your voice. Just sing from your heart. The Lord gave you a voice, in fact, He created you to sound the way you do. Since our God is perfect, and He created what pleased Him, let Him hear you sing, showing Him gratitude for giving you a voice to praise Him.

Psalm 103
Bless the Lord, O my soul;
And all that is within me, bless His holy name!
Bless the Lord, O my soul,
And forget not all His benefits:
Who forgives all your iniquities, Who heals all your diseases.

Think about what this Psalm is saying while you sing. Meditate on what you are singing, instead of how you sound. In order to get more insight with any scripture, you can look at different versions of the scripture. The Amplified or Message translations are good versions to read in order to gain more clarity.

Amplified Version

Bless (affectionately, gratefully praise) the Lord, O my soul; and all that is [deepest] within me, bless His holy name!
Bless (affectionately, gratefully praise) the Lord, O my soul, and forget not [one of] all His benefits–

Who forgives [every one of] all your iniquities, Who heals [each one of] all your diseases

Whenever we bless the Lord with our soul, the deepest place within us, we actually allow God to come into that place, which will bring healing and freedom.

Now, with your heart and mind focusing on the scripture and its meaning, sing the scripture in whatever rhythm and tone. It's your song to the Lord. Don't think about it very much. Trust that the Holy Spirit who lives inside of you will help you sing to the Lord, for He is your Teacher and Guide. Imagine God is right in front you, face to face.

"Let us then approach God's throne of grace with confidence, so that we may receive mercy and find grace to help us in our time of need." ~ Hebrews 4:16

SING the lines of the scripture that you feel comfortable with, a line, or the whole verse. As you sing, you may want to add your own words. Whatever the Holy Spirit leads you to, is what will come out. The more you do this, the more natural it will become.

It is time to sing:

Pray: *"Father, thank you that you said I can come boldly to your throne of grace with confidence. I come confidently, knowing you want me to come to you. Holy Spirit, help me worship in a deeper way. Help me to be free in my worship without restraints. I partner with you Holy Spirit and yield to your leading."*

Next, with your eye of faith, expect the Holy Spirit to do it through you. Begin to sing what you feel comfortable singing, the duration is up to you and the Holy Spirit. However, I have found that when I don't have a set time limit, the more intimate and profound the time of worship becomes.

"Bless the Lord, O my soul;
And all that is within me, bless His holy name! Bless the Lord, O my soul,

And forget not all His benefits:
Who forgives all your iniquities, Who heals all your diseases."

If it was difficult at first, don't worry! Just like with any exercise, it'll feel foreign at first, until you continue to exercise this new principle in your life. Remember, it is a key that will lead you to great victory!

How do you feel?

_____

_____

Was it difficult for you to focus?

_____

_____

You can sing any scripture. Psalms is a great tool. Make the Word of God personal to you and you will see the Word become alive in your life!

> *"So you are no longer a slave, but God's child; and since you are his child, God has made you also an heir."* ~ Galatians 4:7 NIV

What exactly was the transformational power that gave Saul the grace to walk in his God-given purpose and destiny as Paul, an apostle of Jesus Christ? Let's look at the story of Paul on his way to Damascus. Paul was very much set on his opinion of those who followed Christ. He not only hated Christians, but he ordered to have them persecuted and killed (Acts 9). Along the way, he had an encounter that would forever change his mind, his focus, and the direction of his passion and purpose for life.

An encounter with the Lord will do that for every one of us, with one word, one encounter, our mind, focus, direction, and passion can be altered, leading us to our God given purpose. In order to prove God was indeed speaking, Saul's vision was temporarily blinded. I believe it was a prophetic act that revealed the spiritual state of Paul. He was a blind man on a mission and God wanted to restore His sight. He restored His sight in such a way that he never saw in the same context again. His vision was restored and expanded with the ability to see in the spirit as well as in the natural.

Every time we partake of His presence, our spiritual senses are awakened and elevated. When we are awakened (in the spirit, soul, and body) towards the things of God, we begin to live a life of worship. The wonderful thing is, Paul didn't even know to look to God, through Jesus. Jesus interrupted his life and made Himself known. Have you ever been there? I certainly have! Because of the Lord and His amazing mercy, He still chooses those that are blind in their mission, restores their vision with sharper and more dimensional vision, and beckons us closer to intimate encounters. Intimate encounters with God, a place where every need is met and every position that has been forfeited by man can be filled by God Himself. Intimacy with God is the best spiritual posture and can position us to see marvelous works by the hand of God. When we come to the place of true worship, His water, His presence will satisfy and quench our thirst.

If we walk away from worshipping God unchanged and with the same heart as before, we have not worshipped enough. There are many times in my life when choosing to do the right thing was very difficult. The right thing is to deny what I choose for the sake of submitting to His will, His Word. It is then, at that moment of choosing that I am faced with a decision. Do I love the Lord more than what is in front of me? Can I worship Him with the decision to choose Him instead? This is the question He is asking for all those who carry His name: Do you not know I AM enough?" Allow Him to be the Lord of everything, your actions, your words, in what you see, in what you hear, in all you do.

Let's declare: As a daughter of the King, I will worship Him with Praise and my lifestyle.

Reflection: What are some ideas God is giving you about how you can worship Him with your everyday life? Is He asking you to lay anything down in surrender as an act of worship?

Remember to say the prayer out loud so that you can hear what you are praying.

Father, in the name of Jesus, teach me what it means to live a lifestyle of worship. Holy Spirit, stir up the fire, keeping the torch of passion for the LORD lit for all to see. I want to become a torch that will lead others to Your heart. Give me the grace to hear when you are beckoning me to come sit with You and help me structure my days so that I make time for our relationship. I want my soul, spirit, and body to be touched by Your presence, bringing amazing transformation and revealing more of Your character. I want to encounter You more intimately and keep You as the center of my life. I want to see Your power flow through my life as I submit myself to worship You with all that is within me. Teach me how to worship freely. In Jesus name, Amen.

— Chapter 10 —

W- Stay in the Word

Without the Word of God, we cannot renew our mind.

> *"Do not conform to the pattern of this world, but be transformed by the renewing of your mind. Then you will be able to test and approve what God's will is—His good, pleasing and perfect will." ~* Romans 12:2 NIV

If we do not meditate and hear the Word continuously, then the Word cannot come into our hearts. We cannot armor ourselves or raise a standard to the devil without the Word solidly in our lives. Jesus fought the devil with the Word, so we cannot fight without the Word. In addition, if you do not know what standard God wants you to live by, you cannot know who you are IN Christ. Since we live in this world and the purity of our faith is constantly being confronted, we need to be continuously washed in the Word so that our minds line up with Him. When a storm comes, the Word needs to come from within so that you can stand up against the fiery darts of the wicked one. How can we know the Word if we don't study it for ourselves? How can we digest it if we do not consume it regularly?

> *"But He replied, It has been written, Man shall not live and be upheld and sustained by bread alone, but by every word that comes forth from the mouth of God." ~* Matthew 4:4 AMP

Jesus resisted the enemy with the written Word and we must do the same. When we speak the Word with faith in the confidence that it is more powerful than the schemes of satan, satan has no power in the situation. Submitting to the Word, declaring the Word, and combining our declarations with faith, will bring the power of the Holy Spirit, which will cause us to prevail over every attack of the wicked one.

"Take the helmet of salvation and the sword of the Spirit, which is the word of God." ~ Ephesians 6:17 NIV

Since our sword is our weapon, if we do not have the Word in us, we stand defenseless. A helmet surrounds and protects our head. The Word of God surrounds and protects our mind. When we fight with the enemy, we have to allow the Word to protect our mind. It is our job to allow the Word of God to marinate our minds so that we can respond well and protect what has been made rightfully ours by the blood of Jesus.

"In the beginning God created the heavens and the earth. Now the earth was formless and empty, darkness was over the surface of the deep, and the Spirit of God was hovering over the waters And God said, "Let there be light," and there was light. God saw that the light was good, and he separated the light from the darkness. God called the light "day," and the darkness he called "night." And there was evening, and there was morning—the first day." ~ Genesis 1:1-5 NIV

"Then God said, "Let us make mankind in our image, in our likeness, so that they may rule over the fish in the sea and the birds in the sky, over the livestock and all the wild animals, and over all the creatures that move along the ground." ~ Genesis 1:26 NIV

In the beginning God created the heavens and the earth while the Holy Spirit hovered over the water. I believe the Holy Spirit was hovering because He was awaiting commands from Father God. When in your life there are things you are walking through, the Spirit is hovering and Angels are prepared to bring forth the Word that you release. When we declare the Word of God into our circumstances, life is released. Misalignment becomes aligned, light and darkness separate. In your life there are circumstances that appear empty and dark, it doesn't appear there is much life, just like the Father saw an empty and dark place when creation was formed. But, those very areas that seem lifeless are waiting for you, who hold the power of God within, to shine the life producing Word.

Declaring the Word of God has creative power, because life is waiting on the other side. The words that are written in the Word of God are spiritual and are given to you by your covenant with God. We must esteem the Word, because it is our inheritance from God, able to penetrate every situation and circumstance. You are made in the image of God, with a Spirit who is prepared to take dominion over situations as you line up your declarations to the written Word. Genesis 1:26 says, we are called to rule over the creatures, of every kind, both physically and spiritually. The serpent is a creature! The demons are creatures! You are called to bring power and dominion wherever you walk and bring things in alignment with the Word of God.

The Word brings freedoms that nothing else can bring. No written Word can return back to God void.

> "So is my word that goes out from my mouth: It will not return to me empty, but will accomplish what I desire and achieve the purpose for which I sent it." ~ Isaiah 55:11 NIV

Never, ever accept defeat in your life! When you appear defeated, know it is not over. When Jesus was nailed to the cross, it appeared to be over, but no one was ready for the power of the Holy Spirit that would raise Him from the dead. Your situation is not over. The Holy Spirit will bring the Word of God to pass. The Lord has left us His Word so that when we speak what He has spoken, His power is released. As God saw His Word come to pass in creation—He will see to it that when you speak the Word, the Holy Spirit will bring it to pass. The earth was empty until God said! Your situation is empty until you say the Word. Our job is to speak the Word.

"In the beginning was the Word, and the Word was with God, and the Word was God. He was with God in the beginning. Through him all things were made; without him nothing was made that has been made. In him was life, and that life was the light of all mankind. The light shines in the darkness, and the darkness has not overcome it There was a man sent from God whose name was John. He came as a witness to testify concerning that light, so that through him all might believe. (It is God's will for ALL to believe). *He himself was not the light; he came only as a witness to the light. The true light that gives light to everyone was coming into the world. He was in the world, and though the world was made through him, the world did not recognize him. He came to that which was his own, but his own did not receive him. Yet to all who did receive him, to those who believed in his name, he gave the right to become children of God— children born not of natural descent, nor of human decision or a husband's will, but born of God."* ~ John 1:1-13 NIV

Isn't it amazing that although the world was created through Jesus Christ, the world did not recognize Him. Even His own family rejected Him. Know this, when God sends you to a place, the people may not recognize you were sent by God. They may not recognize the anointing on your life, but when the appointed time comes, God will make His plan known. You just keep on walking, whether you are received or not. If God called you there, you are not walking alone. The enemy wants you to think you heard wrong, but if Jesus went through it, we must expect it, too.

"The Word became flesh and made his dwelling among us. We have seen his glory, the glory of the one and only Son, who came from the Father, full of grace and truth." ~ John 1:14 NIV

The Word is Jesus. If we don't have the Word in us, then we cannot have Jesus in us. The Word—Jesus- becomes alive when we apply the Word in our lives.

"So shall they fear the name of the Lord from the west, And His glory from the rising of the sun; When the enemy comes in like a flood, The Spirit of the Lord will lift up a standard against him." ~ Isaiah 59:19 NKJV

Who does the Spirit of God raise up a standard against? The enemy! What is the standard? His Word! Who is the Standard? Jesus Christ!

If I want to measure something, I need the appropriate measuring device, a ruler, tape measure, etc. I would hold the measuring device next to what I was measuring in order to obtain the accurate measurement. In any situation, I can hold the measurement or standard of the Word. If it does not hold up to its standard, I can speak the Word over the situation until it does. When the enemy comes, the Word is the measuring stick. Don't accept anything less!

The order of the Godhead is: Father God is the Mastermind. Jesus is the One who speaks the plan. The Holy Spirit is the One who brings it to pass. If we want our lives to be fruitful and victorious—we must speak what Jesus speaks----the WORD. The Holy Spirit will see to it that the standard is raised for our benefit. Having the Word in our lives—is having Jesus in our lives. It's taking communion with Him, when we utilize His Word, utilizing the gift He has given us.

We have to know the Word to know who we are in Christ. We need to preach to ourselves. We need to tell ourselves to "get over ourselves." No human person knows our thoughts better than ourselves. Therefore, we know our weaknesses. Speak the Word that is relevant to those weaknesses. If we don't have the Word in us— then we cannot measure our motives. Since we live in this world, we need to be continuously washed in the Word so that our minds are lined up with the Word. We do not naturally crave what God craves. When a tree is first planted, it needs to be anchored to the ground so that when a storm comes, it will remain standing with strength. In order for us to remain standing in the storms of life, we must be "anchored" to the Word with it in our hearts so that we can stand up against the fiery darts of the wicked one.

When my husband and I bought our first house, we bought the largest tree we could afford for our front yard, which was a puny little tree, and planted it. In order for a tree to grow up strong and withstand the storms in its immature state, it must be anchored and staked to the ground on both sides, with ropes securing it. The reason for this is when the strong winds blow, the tree won't collapse. The pressure of the wind actually causes the roots of the tree to dig deeper into the soil. When the strong winds come, gardeners will tell you that the roots of the tree actually go deeper into the soil and the resistance actually makes the tree stronger. If we can recognize that we are like "trees" planted in the "soil" of Jesus Christ, we will understand that when the winds and storms come, our roots become stronger and what used to topple us over, no longer will. We can get stronger and stronger and grow from Glory to Glory, because we recognize who sustains our roots. Here is an illustration of how we can react with the Word of God.

I had developed a friendship with a young lady who lived with her boyfriend a couple of houses away. I had it in my heart to buy her a bible and planned on giving it to her as a gift. It sat on my desk waiting for the perfect opportunity to give it to her. It was a hot day as I was dancing to my Zumba DVD. I glanced outside the window and saw she was moving out, obviously breaking up with her boyfriend. I hurried to give her the gift. Next door to my home, lived a Mormon family who had a guest leaving and was standing in the area I was crossing. As I was running down the sidewalk, I stepped on a rock and tripped and fell on the hot asphalt. I felt my ankle snap and the pain was almost unbearable. The first words out of the guest's mouth were, "Oh no, did you break your ankle?" (The enemy wants us to agree with his attacks when we are vulnerable.) Praise God, that I was saturated with the Word. I had soaked in His presence prior to this incident.

My response, as quickly as she retorted the question was, "No weapon formed against me shall prosper. I am healed in Jesus name." I even surprised myself that the words coming out of my mouth were so opposite of the pain that I felt. As I got up, I started to hobble to the mission, which was to give my friend a Bible. By the time our conversation had finished, the pain had left, and I felt much better. I still had scrapes on my leg, but my ankle was healed! If the Word had not been in my heart, I am convinced the outcome would have been much different. Darts from the enemy will be sent your way, but when you have the Word in your heart, you have protection and are not bare handed and able to fight back!

The Word has to be the reaction to our circumstances.... if the Word is not in us, then we have nothing to draw from. Like the caterpillar needs to eat and eat—we must be nourished continuously from the Word of God.

> *"It is written, 'Man shall not live by bread alone, but by every word that proceeds from the mouth of God.'"* ~ Matthew 4:4 NIV

When someone is just beginning to study the Word of God, I recommend to read it slowly and carefully, fully digesting what you are reading, even if it is only one verse at a time. In order for you to have complete understanding, you must invite the Holy Spirit to partner with you and teach you, and eat slowly. When we try to read a large content of scriptures, especially when just beginning, it is like gorging ourselves with food. We are mindlessly eating. In order to get good nutrition and digestion, we must eat food with purpose and eat slowly. We can't read the Bible like we do any other book, each word is specifically chosen to be the written Word of God, like a love letter in order for Him to reveal Himself. How amazing! Read the scriptures in chunks and really meditate on it. For me, I begin my scripture reading with a prayer like this, *"Holy Spirit, I invite You to teach me and give me Your revelation. Give me the nuggets you want me to receive today. In Jesus name."*

Not long ago, I was in a prayer circle and the Lord had given someone a vision of a cow. The cow was chewing. I realized God wants us to chew His Word like cows chew cud. The cud is actually chewed hay that is regurgitated and then chewed more. It is chewed continuously until it is digested. By chewing cud, the cow is able to receive the nutrition from the hay in its fullest form. We need to receive the Word daily and really "chew on it" throughout the day, meditate on those studied scriptures and "chew on it" some more. Meditating on the Word like this will cause the Word to become alive in your life and drop into your heart's reservoir so that you can bring it forth as a weapon when the time is needed.... Just like Jesus.

Let's declare: *"To fight satan, I must have the Word in me, and speak it."*

The Word of God can become our standard of how we care for ourselves, how to raise the standard in our homes, our relationships, what we allow in our lives and so on. Abiding in the parameters of the Word of God brings protection like nothing else.

Let's declare: *"I have the power of the living God to speak what He speaks and see it come to pass. To fight against satan, I must have the Word in ME and speak it. When I speak the Word of God over my situation, the power of God is released and every situation must bow at the name of Jesus."*

Remember to say the prayer out loud so that you can hear what you are praying.

Father, in the name of Jesus, give me a hunger for Your Word, allowing it to become the standard in which I live by. Holy Spirit, teach me more revelation from the Word as I apply it in my life. I don't want anything stolen or bypassed in my life. Therefore, I want to submit myself to Your Word, and allow it to become alive in me. Bless You Lord, for the gift of Your Word, for it is my inheritance through your Son. In Jesus name, Amen

—Chapter 11—

E-Exercising Servanthood

Serving does not always come naturally. Most of us want to serve, but sometimes as women, we can get slavery and serving mixed up. Many times we want to do everything people request of us. But, God is not asking us to do everything... He just wants our "yes" to serve in the areas He is requesting. When I say "serving", I do not want anyone to go and put their names on every volunteer sheet that comes their way. An exhausted woman becomes empty quite quickly, and that is not God's intent. Without a healthy mindset, serving can be done by manipulation (getting something out of return), or for seeking approval from others. We must exercise true servanthood, by being like Christ— and serving others.... out of obedience to the LORD.

> *"God has given each of you a gift from his great variety of spiritual gifts. Use them well to serve one another."* ~1 Peter 4:10 NLT

The level of revelation we have of who Jesus Christ is to us personally, determines how much of our lives we are willing to lay down and surrender. I am completely convinced that God searches for those that are willing to allow Him to change them, so that He can change circumstances. When you receive His love, you naturally want to do something for Him. When you realize what He purchased with His blood for you, you want to serve Him. It is satan's bait to have us focus on ourselves. This keeps us from the blessings that serving Christ, by serving others offers.

The enemy (satan) wants us to focus on offense, rebelliousness, selfishness, and strife. But, NO! You are not made in satan's image;

you are made in God's image.... The greater One lives in you! You have something inside of you, that God wants to use to bless someone else. You are a gift, but not for yourself. You have value! You have a position on the team of Jesus Christ to fill!

In order to be trusted with more, you must be faithful with little. You have to learn to do, when you don't feel like it. Never forget, obedience is better than sacrifice! You see, your works won't get you into the Kingdom of God. Accepting the blood of Jesus and living with Him as your Lord, gives you access into those gates. The works you do unto Him NOW, reveals your love and adoration to Him to the world.

Does satan know how much you and I love the Lord by how we live our lives and how we choose to spend our time? If your life was video-recorded, would how you use your time and your gifts display your love for God? Does what you take the time to participate in reflect who you honor and love? Devotion is seen in action, not words. Christianity is seen in our fruit; by the way we *live*. We can all make some adjustments to reveal our love for the Lord more clearly. The grace of God is willing to meet us. All we have to do is ask and believe. Belief that we received grace looks like action in place. The more we do for others, the less we think of ourselves. Therefore, we are being a true witness and testament to the character of Christ when we serve others.

> *"This service that you perform is not only supplying the needs of the Lord's people but is also overflowing in many expressions of thanks to God."* ~ 2 Corinthians 9:12 NIV

When you serve, you bring glory to God—You give people the opportunity to glorify God. By serving them, they are thankful to Him for your obedience. Here is an illustration in my life of serving with obedience.

While grocery shopping at Costco, I felt the prompting of the Holy Spirit to buy a 15-pound bag of chicken breast for our neighbor. I thought this was a very odd prompting, because I didn't think they were lacking money for groceries. It made no sense to me at all to take them raw chicken. I felt very silly about randomly taking a large bag of frozen chicken breasts across to my neighbors. I was just learning how to discern the voice of God, and was worried I would make a mistake. After my time of grocery shopping, I pulled into our driveway. Looking through the rear view mirror, I saw that very neighbor with her trunk opened, unloading all of her just bought groceries. My heart dropped, thinking I had totally missed it.

After putting my groceries away, I recall asking the Lord repeatedly to please confirm if I had understood correctly. He was quiet, very quiet, as if He was giving me a choice to give or not give, to be obedient or disobedient. I decided to get over myself and take this bag of chicken across the street. Never had I had such a long conversation in my mind about chicken!!! So, in my rationale, I thought, "Let me get a bag large enough to conceal this chicken, because if I'm wrong, maybe I don't even have to let her know what's in the bag." But, I didn't have a bag big enough to conceal it.

I felt so silly! "I'll just prompt her with some random questions about chicken." Really? You see, at the time, we lived in the type of community where people competed against each other to have the best of everything. Most neighbors were not vulnerable with each other. I also didn't want to offend her, and here I was, with this job from God, to deliver a huge bag of frozen chicken. I started to doubt my ability to hear God's voice. As I was crossing the street, the Holy Spirit reminded me that Peter denied Jesus three times, but when the Holy Spirit came, he led over 3,000 people to the Lord because the Holy Spirit filled him with courage and boldness (Acts 2).

As I walked, I said, "Holy Spirit, if you showed up for Peter, you'll certainly show up for me, even if it is just chicken!" Since I was new at listening to the voice of God, my heart felt as if it would beat out of my chest waiting for the door to be answered. My neighbor opened the door, and her eyes went straight to that bag of raw, frozen chicken. "Hi Monica, what do you have there?" As nervous as I was just minutes before, Love took over at that moment. The words just flowed right out, "I was grocery shopping and felt compelled by God to bring this bag of chicken to you all. I know I see a lot of groceries being unloaded out of your car, but still, I really perceive God wanting me to give you this chicken."

She responded, as tears filled her eyes, "I went to the grocery store and spent so much time shopping and getting all the things we needed, and I was so upset when I got home because I forgot to buy chicken! I was so mad at myself for forgetting because I ran out of time and my flight leaves soon and I need to leave our family with food. It's been so hard. I've been praying so much for God to answer my prayers, and I've been feeling as if He just isn't listening."

I was so grateful I chose to listen! I was able to minister God's love to her, proving God listens to her and loves her immensely! If God can talk to me while shopping at Costco, so that He can show up and fill a need, He will show up for your needs and partner with you to fulfill the needs of others. All the while, increasing your faith in Him that He is GOOD! I have never questioned His prompting again! Because I obeyed God, she was able to glorify God with her gratitude and her faith was ignited! When you feel the prompting of the Lord, GO FOR IT! You don't know what praise to God is attached to your obedience and how it impacts another.

As wives, our primary calling is to our husbands and children. The overflow of our time and efforts are for those around us. Where is He calling you to serve? There is a time and a season for everything. If all He calls you to do is bring cookies to the newcomers, do it unto Him. If He wants you to help with ushering or the youth ministry at your church, do it unto Him! If He has you to teach or host a bible study, do it unto Him! Ask Him, "Lord, where can I serve you?" Since part of our worship is to tithe so that there would be spiritual food in the house, then we must also serve others as part of our worship.

As a homeschool mother, I did not have the time nor the desire to run the home by myself. There are many chores that need to be done in a home. I have taught my children that we are a team. I cannot run the household without them. They are crucial to our efficiency. The congregation is crucial to the efficiency of the ministry. We share the load of work in our home and help each other, even when it is not a job assigned to us. Because, that is what a good team player does. In my family, we all resemble each other. Our facial features and mannerisms are similar. In order to be a legitimate child of God, we need to resemble the character and actions of Jesus, and Jesus laid His life down to serve.

Challenge: Ask the Lord to help you recognize where He is calling you to serve HIM.

_____

_____

_____

"By the grace God has given me, I laid a foundation as a wise builder, and someone else is building on it. But each one should build with care. For no one can lay any foundation other than the one already laid, which is Jesus Christ. If anyone builds on this foundation using gold, silver, costly stones, wood, hay or straw, their work will be shown for what it is, because the Day will bring it to light. It will be revealed with fire, and the fire will test the quality of each person's work. If what has been built survives, the builder will receive a reward. If it is burned up,

the builder will suffer loss but yet will be saved—even though only as one escaping through the flames." ~ 1 Corinthians 3:10-15

I like the Message translation of 1 Corinthians 3:10-15.

"Or, to put it another way, you are God's house. Using the gift God gave me as a good architect, I designed blueprints; Apollos is putting up the walls. Let each carpenter who comes on the job take care to build on the foundation! Remember, there is only one foundation, the one already laid: Jesus Christ. Take particular care in picking out your building materials. Eventually there is going to be an inspection. If you use cheap or inferior materials, you'll be found out. The inspection will be thorough and rigorous. You won't get by with a thing. If your work passes inspection, fine; if it doesn't, your part of the building will be torn out and started over. But you won't be torn out; you'll survive—but just barely."

What we do for the Lord must be built on the foundation of Jesus Christ, and what we do must be done because He has begun the work and will carry it on through us. The fire is the representation of the purity within our heart, the motive behind what we do. Many times our schedules are solidly booked, and although we might be doing awesome things for the Lord, we may be doing it for the wrong reasons, to be known or to build an image. Applause from people can feel so good to those who have a need for validation. If we stay quiet long enough in the presence of the LORD, we can hear Him validate us, approve us, and applaud us. Many times, we would never think to even seek Him for validation and applause. He longs for us to hear His voice as He encourages us. God is a consuming fire and only those things that are pure will go unburned.

Imagine a precious metal, just found in the ground, being placed in the heat of the fire. All impurities will melt, for they cannot stand in the fire. A refiner keeps the gold in the hot flames until the dross melts off the preciousness of the metal, while being molded into the creation of the refiner. The gold is held in the fire until the refiner sees his reflection, for that is when he knows the work is complete. When the refiner can see his reflection, he knows the gold is prepared for the purpose in which he was intending it for. Father God is the REFINER.

The amount of time we spend on earth is only a vapor compared to eternity. POOF and it's gone! I see many people serving God out of the wrong motives---many are serving God out of feeling condemnation from others or trying to get people or even God to notice them. I have been there, too! Too often our homes get out of order, because we are saying "yes" to every work that comes our way. Our families, our first mission field, suffer neglect when we do not put them in proper order. If my husband and my children do not see what I preach, I am only a hypocrite with a heart of a Pharisee. Even if I won one million souls to the Kingdom of God, what would that merit, if I lost my children to the devil?

I want my children to encounter God while my life reflects the beckoning to His heart. I asked God once, "What kind of works gets burned up in the fire? I don't want any of my "works" to go unnecessary." He by His grace, answered---"The reason My people's works get burned up is because they stopped doing them out of Love and obedience to ME." Anytime our focus is not Love for our God, our works get burned up. LOVE HAS TO BE THE MOTIVATOR AND THE FOCUS. Obedience follows His love. When we recognize His love, His love will compel us to serve Him lavishly.

Everyone has a position that needs to be filled on the team. Whether you usher, make cookies, empty the trash can, no matter what you do, do it unto Him. Ask the Holy Spirit to guide you, as how you can serve Him daily and how He would like you to serve in His Church. Speak to someone in your church as to how you can get involved, or you may be called to another community work. Don't delay! Do it while you feel prompted. We should always make sure to be obedient to what He tells us while we are under His anointing, otherwise, we can put off, and the moment ceases.

He can do amazing things with our humble "yes". The Word says Jesus is the Head of the Body of Christ.

> *"And He is the head of the body, the church; he is the beginning and the firstborn from among the dead, so that in everything he might have the supremacy."* ~ Colossians 1:18 NIV

We can't be a body without every part of the Body coming together doing their part. I heard Bill Johnson of Bethel Church in Redding, California, say, "Jesus is coming for a Body who is in equal proportion to the Head."

I was really meditating on that quote when I had a dream of the most distorted baby I had ever seen. This baby had a humongous head, and a teeny, tiny body; no symmetry whatsoever. It was not cute. I felt God say 'I am bringing My Church to become equal to the proportion of My Head." The Body can only follow the Head when it is attached to the Head. A detached body is not alive. That is why we must remember, we are the extension of Jesus Christ. Jesus Christ has said "It is Finished." Therefore, as His extension, (His arms, His legs, etc.) we are called to represent Him on earth in obedience.

> *"For even the Son of Man did not come to be served, but to serve, and to give his life as a ransom for many."* ~ Mark 10:45 NIV

In the amazing story of Hosea, Hosea the prophet is told by God to go and marry a prostitute named Gomer. This prostitute continues to have adulterous relationships and defile their marital covenant over and over again. Because of this great pain, Hosea understands how God feels when His people turn their back on Him and choose to give their adoration and attention to false gods. Gomer the prostitute leaves Hosea to return back to the only life she finds familiar, prostitution. In the process, her life is held for ransom at an auction, like cattle.

Gomer had willingly chosen to return back to the destructive lifestyle she was brought out of. God tells Hosea to go and buy her back and bring her back to his home to live with him as his wife. Hosea gives everything he has to go and purchase freedom for the one who had continuously abused and dishonored their covenant. How many times in our lives do we return back to our old ways? Sometimes, we revert back to responses from our old lifestyle, like Gomer. What's so awesome is Jesus Christ, our Beloved, the Lover of our soul, our Groom, comes back for us.

Many times we forget that we have been purchased, ransomed by the blood of the KING. We have been bought with a price. If we can truly recognize His blood is sufficient for all that we need, we can continue to abide in the spirit of resurrection. Allowing it to flow in and through us, knowing who we are and never believing anything less. I recognize every time I was blindsided by the enemy has been a result of me losing sight of who purchased my freedom and whose power lives inside of me. Let's walk in His freedom by serving Him with all that we possess.

At the Last supper, before Jesus was taken to be crucified, he spoke to His disciples and said, "Take and eat, THIS IS MY BODY." He gave everything He had! Up to His last breath. Up until all He had to give was His very Flesh. His entire life on earth was lived serving mankind. He gave up His body by shedding it because of His devotion to the Father. He came to teach us love, compassion, discipleship, discipline, faith, and so many other things that we can't possibly list them all. HE served His Father up until His last human breath- when He spoke to the Father and said, "IT IS FINISHED."

When we eat something nutritious it actually goes into our system to give life. When we eat the bread and take communion, we are actually taking resurrecting life to produce life inside of our spirit, as well as body. When Jesus said, "It is finished", He meant the mission was completed. We do not need to do anything but receive. When He completed the work, He gave us everything we need to equip us for the great work He has called us to and ENJOY it. What an absolute gift! The mission of God for the salvation of mankind was done—He lived His life as one on a mission to accomplish the greatest act in history. His life not only brought salvation to those that believe and live for Him, but His life came to teach us how to live and then die, causing us to become resurrected so that we may live with Him for all eternity.

What are we willing to live for? What are we willing to die for? Our Daddy God isn't asking us to shed our blood and get crucified. He is only asking us to allow Him to transform us by removing from us the things that bring destruction so that He can partner with us to bring the same transformation to others.

Let's declare: "*I am designed like no one else, I am gifted for His service.*"

Remember to say the prayer out loud so that you can hear what you are praying.

Father, help me to submit to serving where you are calling me in this season. Let me serve You with a joyful and willing heart, not for rewards or recognition, but only to reveal I want to live as Jesus Christ lived on earth. Help me to trust You as You lead me to serve, knowing You will provide all that I need. Increase my understanding of what it looks like to serve with a heart that is pure and open my ears to hear your approval of me. Help me live a life that is pleasing and give me the grace to enjoy the journey. Thank you, Jesus Christ, for giving us the perfect display of love as you came to serve the Father. Holy Spirit, I ask You to lead me to serve only what I hear you lead me to do, but mostly give me joy to serve those I am called to first. In Jesus name, Amen.

—Chapter 12—

R- Representing the Kingdom

God is looking for people who will allow Him to bring His character and His presence into situations so that transformation comes. Through the darkness, from an aerial view, God is calling His people to pray, but bring forth action as well. The greatest evidence that one can reveal of the transformation they have received from God is revealed in our actions. When people recognize the change you have gone through, they will witness God in action.

Representative: standing or acting for another, especially through delegated authority

Let's declare: *"I have delegated authority."*

> *"We are therefore Christ's ambassadors, as though God were making his appeal through us. We implore you on Christ's behalf: Be reconciled to God."* ~ 2 Corinthians 5:20 NIV

Since God Himself lives in those that love Him, we should want all people to be reconciled to Him. As His representatives, we will either help people desire Him or repel them. We will either attract them to the flame or swat them away. Our actions may be the only "Jesus" they will ever meet.

> *"Therefore, come out from them and be separate, says the Lord. Touch no unclean thing, and I will receive you."* ~2 Corinthians 6:17 NIV

"Depart, depart, go out from there! Touch no unclean thing! Come out from it and be pure, you who carry the vessels of the LORD." ~ Isaiah 52:11 NKJV

In other words, He is saying, "COME OUT! Come out! Do not conform to the world. Come out of your oppression, come out! Do not partake in what the world partakes in. Come out from it and crave what I crave, be pure, you who carry my Spirit. You, whom I want to use to impart my Spirit onto others."

If we don't reveal the true nature of Jesus Christ by discipling our children, who will disciple them? If we can't reveal His nature by how we love and live, how will they see Him? If we don't experience Him, how can we reveal Him? If we are not disciplined enough to change the television channel, change the radio station, or remove ourselves from atmospheres that are destructive, how will our children learn to do it on their own? How can we expect from our children what we are not willing to do ourselves? I have to *choose* to keep a constant remembrance of who I represent and I cannot partake in an action the Word says not to partake in, if I want to see freedom in the lives of those I love and called to raise up. To truly parent a child in the ways of God means we model Him, despite how we feel.

We won't get anywhere by preaching to people with a finger in their face. God's message is always to draw from love and kindness by sharing with people who they are: Loved and sought after by God Himself. Who we serve and represent will be evident in our actions and speech. When the opportunity to have a fit or a tantrum arises, we have to have a plan of how we will respond before it happens because sooner or later, someone is going to upset us. Our response is our choice. We serve God, by the actions we choose, not only when it comes easily. As a matter of fact, who we serve is seen in the choices we make when it is most difficult. Our actions are a witness to whom we are serving, and are a witness to our children and the world.

"Blessed are the peacemakers, for they shall be called sons of God." ~ Matthew 5:9 NKJV

Under "**peacemaker**" in the Webster's dictionary, are the synonyms "intercessor & interceder." A related word for peacemaker is ambassador.

Intercession is defined as: prayer, petition, or entreaty in favor of another.

Intercede is: to intervene between parties with a view to reconciling differences.

Once you have a relationship with Jesus Christ, many won't understand you anymore. But, although they can't understand or recognize you, they will know who to go to for prayer when they have a need. You may also find that because of your new transformation, you may now be excluded from certain events with people you love. But, if you allow yourself to take the position as the assigned ambassador and INTERCESSOR, you will be able to bring the power of transformation to them.

The Great Holy Spirit wants to partner with us to infiltrate those who are in our area of influence. There are many things in our families that God did not call to be there, and He is calling one person, one seed, to be transformed so that He can penetrate the atmosphere with Light and Life. Whether you are physically present in their activities holds no bounds, your prayers and what you deposit in the people when they are with you, are enough to bring the witness of Light and Love.

Many Christians that I know put more emphasis on loving their brothers and sisters in the church than they do with their brothers and sisters by blood that have not come into the Body of Christ, yet. Many Christians labor for those they attend church with and sweep their family members under the rug. I believe wholeheartedly we have to be strategic to become peacemakers between God and the "tribe" we were born into. You were born into a family for the sake of bringing transformation in the Spirit before it is revealed in the physical sense.

If you are adopted, you were placed in the family for the same reasons. God partners with people to work through them so that He can bring His life to circumstances. Especially if you are one of the first ones God has pulled out of traditional religion. God has called you to become like Moses, who led the people to their Promised Land. You may be the only "light" that's available, but God is BIG ENOUGH, and His Light will shine through you even in the darkest and most difficult places. When we love enough to pray for someone else, God will help us to bring peace in the middle of conflict. As an ambassador of Christ, we must bring peace—and quench the fires among us.

When destructive fires are going on around you, whether they involve you or not, it is important to remember, that if you are just standing by observing, you are not being a peacemaker. For example, if you are at work and there is gossip, or neighbors are angry at each other, or family members are against each other, take the situations to God. He may or may not want you to be used as an instrument to bring order to chaos. When we love enough to pray for favor for someone else, God will help us bring peace in the middle of conflict. As an ambassador of Heaven, we must bring the power of the Holy Spirit and quench the fiery darts of satan. Now, this takes much strategy. I believe because of grace and mercy, there comes a time after separation, that God will give you strategic ways to reveal Himself to those that are more difficult to love, because His will is that not anyone should perish, but have everlasting life.

When your family is not walking with God or you have been broken by your family, there may be a time when God leads you to separate from the atmosphere for a time, so that He can further your process of healing. After you are further along, ideas of acts of love, mercy, grace, and kindness will be given to you as strategies to witness to them and allow you to partner with God as an extension of Jesus Christ. When we return to closer fellowship with our families after being healed, we can be spiritually guarded, able to guard our hearts, so that what is said about us, (baits of satan) rolls right off of our backs.

Jesus Christ did not allow anyone or anything to take Him from the mission of the Father. You can imagine when Mary and Joseph were walking on their way home only to find Jesus, being twelve years old, was not with them and He had remained teaching in the Synagogue. Can you imagine traveling by foot for days, and then discovering your twelve-year-old is not with you? Can you imagine how fearful and then angry you might be? Can you imagine the audacity of Jesus, after being questioned about his absence, answered, "Wouldn't you know I would be about my Father's business?" He didn't allow emotions to drive Him.

How about the man who wanted to leave and go bury his father in Luke 9:59-60? Jesus answered him, *"Let the dead bury the dead."* That may seem very cold, but we need to recognize the perspective of the Kingdom is always more interested in the affairs of eternity. What is on the heart of the Kingdom, which is the heart of the Father? When we get Heavens perspective, we will realize some of the things that drives us and compels us are actually not as important as we think they are.

If we choose to go higher to acquire a new perspective by leaving the ground level view (emotional perspective) and get the aerial view (God's point of view), we will be able to see clearer, and recognize what is on the heart of God. When we get His perspective, we can allow God to heal our wounds, and we can see things through His perfect vision. Be mindful of what you put your time into and what you invest in. Ask God when to step in and when to step away. God will call you back in a strategic manner to the same places He took you from, in order to reveal Himself and bring freedom to others.

A peacemaker extinguishes the fires that she witnesses by asking God for His strategy and His heart. If a firefighter who was off duty was the first one to notice a fire, we would expect him to do what he was trained to do, while waiting for the authorities. We would hope that he would not just pass by ignoring it, right? He would have to see to it that no one got hurt while waiting for the team of firefighters. If someone who was capable didn't take these actions and ignored the fire, they would be accused of neglect. When we see fires around us, we have to remember that we have the "authority", the Living God inside of us, and His precious Holy Spirit who is our "water hose."

We must extinguish the fires around us with prayer, use gentleness towards people, and utilize discernment for the right words. As one speaks negatively, the fire inside of them and around them will grow. If you stand and listen to complaints, gossip, or any type of negativity, and not attempt to extinguish the fires by encouraging the person to give grace to the other, then you are adding fuel to the fire and responsible for neglecting your position as an ambassador of the Kingdom of God.

When you have that special somebody who loves to gossip or complain, redirect them, or express statements of grace towards whomever they are complaining about. Nothing irritated me more than when I would gossip and complain and a "goody goody" would say, "Well, you never know what's going on in their life to make them respond like that" or "we just never know what it's like to walk in someone else's shoes. Let's be grateful for what we have, because people everywhere are hurting." Even though it annoyed me, it sure made me shut my mouth! Gossip and complaining are infectious, if you don't shut it up when you're around, it will rub off on you. Shut it up before it comes on you to steal your joy.

As it is said, "You are what you eat." Just as this is true for our physical bodies, it is true of our spiritual bodies. If we partake in what the world partakes in, we will look just like the world. As we grow in Him, He will guide us to become more like Him every day. If we allow a negative habit to starve, it will no longer have a source of life. It takes twenty-one days to make or break a habit. If we indulge in movies, music, friendships, and habits, that do not strengthen our spirits, then we are not becoming more like Jesus and we are not living life as daughters, but one rejecting Him as our Father.

"This is how we know who the children of God are and who the children of the devil are: Anyone who does not do what is right is not God's child; nor is anyone who does not love their brother."~ 1 John 3:10 NIV

Just like when I begin a new diet, it is up to me to keep myself in an atmosphere that will encourage discipline to allow those new habits and endurance to increase and strengthen, so that I can actually be what I have said I want to be. Also, the love of the brother is so important to God because it is the witness of our love that sets us apart from those who do not know God. Like a moth to the flame, they shall be compelled by our Love. The peacemakers of God are called to be on a pursuit of love to bring the peace of God to not only the brothers and sisters in the faith, but also to those that have not come into the family of faith yet. God wants us to extend grace, mercy, and love, for if we do not, how will they know us? How will they know He who has sent us?

Not long ago, two young men came to our front door asking to mow our yard. We had a large yard and he requested only $20. Of course, I couldn't just give him $20, because it involved a lot of labor. Our backyard was also on an incline. Although I agreed to the $20, I wanted to give him more after the job was complete. After he finished and I paid him, I asked him if I could pray with him about anything. With dirt smeared on his face and clothes, he looked at me quite strange and agreed. He didn't have a special request, so I just prayed that God would bless them, expand their business, and bless all that he put his hands to, never knowing lack, in Jesus name. I simply prayed love, nothing in return.

Two weeks later, I texted them requesting their work again. He asked me if he could return on Easter Sunday. I responded, "Easter Sunday??" He asked me to leave a check under the door mat, and he would get it when he came. He explained he did not celebrate Easter Sunday. When he returned another time, I walked out of our house to see him working on two different neighbor's yards. So I yelled out "I see God has you pretty busy?" He smiled and said, "YES!" Whenever he or any other worker came, I offered them cold drinks and even meals at times.

Everything we do is a witness to who we love. God will lead you as you allow Him. Every person who you come in contact with, there is an opportunity to reveal Jesus and how GOOD the FATHER IS. With every opportunity, extend the love that you have been given. Love covers and makes a difference! When we step out a little bit more to reveal He who lives inside of us, He can't be missed! Our true witness is seen in what we do, not what we say. What are you willing to do to reveal you care about people?

Let's declare: *"As His daughter, I crave and love those things He craves and loves."*

What are the things we want to focus on and allow in our spirits?

Let's look at Philippians 4:8!

> *"Finally, brothers and sisters, whatever is true, whatever is noble, admirable--if anything is excellent or praiseworthy-- think about such things."*

I heard Mike Murdock, founder of The Wisdom Center, say, "You were given your mouth to tell your mind to be quiet." In other words, whatever we allow our minds to meditate on will eventually come out of our mouths and on display for the world to witness. If we ponder how mad we are at someone—eventually, we will want to walk up to them and slap them. The more we concentrate on a problem, the more irritated we become. The more we focus on what someone is not doing right, the more frustrated we become with them. If we could just reposition our minds and choose to look at the good things within others or within situations, our minds could become a place for peace to reside by allowing the grace of God in and through us. A grateful heart will allow transformation in any situation. If we stop negative thoughts as soon as they start by asking God to help us submit to His love and ask and expect Him to fill us with grace so that we can love others, the poisonous thoughts won't have a breeding ground to continue. This is especially helpful for those that have frequent head pain, migraines, headaches, etc.

During a counseling session with a couple, the husband admitted he was having a difficult time with pornography. I explained how our thoughts become the seed to the sin, opened by a gate (your eyes are a gate). The seeds are planted subtly. So subtly, you hardly realize it's there. For instance, a man could be at the gas station while a woman is bending over getting something out of her car. He could choose at that moment to look another direction and focus on thoughts towards God, or he can continue to feast his eyes on this woman and think about her.

The seed begins to take root as he ponders on her throughout the day. Eventually, these thoughts begin to grow and germinate and leads further down the path towards sexual perversion, to become an unquenchable desire for lust. This is why it is very important that we stop the seed at the moment it tries to come in our thought lives. Be quick to take every thought captive, so that you can stand firm against the schemes of satan. To take captive every thought, means you restrain the thought. You don't allow it to flow into your mind. You contain it, like behind prison bars. If it does not line up with the Word of God and take you towards the path you want to go, (FREEDOM) stand up against it.

Declare with your mouth: *"This is not my thought. I will not take ownership of it. Father, I submit my mind and thoughts to you. I will choose to meditate on thoughts that produce life. I yield to you, in Jesus name."*

> *"We demolish arguments and every pretension that sets itself up against the knowledge of God, and we take captive every thought to make it obedient to Christ."* ~ 2 Corinthians 10:5 NIV

What is the reason for your freedom, besides His love? Why does He want you to be transformed and have a renewed mind, other than for your own benefit? You didn't choose Him, He chose YOU. Why did God choose you? So many people still have not come to God. Why did He choose to call you forward?

> *"No one can come to Me unless the Father who sent me draws them, and I will raise them up at the last day."* ~ John 6:44 NIV

> *"The Spirit of the Lord is on me, because he has anointed me to preach good news to the poor. He has sent me to proclaim freedom for the prisoners and recovery of sight for the blind, to set the oppressed free, to proclaim the year of the Lord's favor."* ~ Luke 4:18 NIV

God has called you to look for those that need His Good News, freedom, and someone to hold their hand as they walk through transformation. They need someone to show them there is another way, a way that produces life and freedom. Since God is the Father of fathers, and He cared so much about extending His family, He sent His son, who is God Himself, to die such a gruesome death, so that you and I could accept that He was God. Our sins are erased because of His obedience and His love. GOD TRULY CARES whether you love Him enough to bring people with you. Do we care for His family, like He does? If so, who is He calling you to help become free? Who is God calling you to inspire by your stories of hope? Who has God called you to deposit seeds of your time by sowing love and prayer? Who can you impact because of your life and inspire them to come along and join you in the adventure of walking with God?

The enemy (satan) has caused women to focus on our own concerns in order to keep us restrained. As long as we are restrained by fear, intimidation, inferiority, or shame, etc., we cannot love those around us. Sometimes we become so isolated and engulfed in our own lives, we fail to connect with those that are hurting because it requires the investment of time. When we see a woman who seems to be more "pulled together", we allow a wedge to be built between us. Those inadequacies make one bitter, frustrated, and alone. People who don't live in His love are shackled by their past identifying them.

In the game of basketball, if someone is playing the position of defense, their job is to prevent the other team from scoring. Many times this is what we do to other women. We get jealous of each other when the other "scores". We want to be the one who "scores" the points. How? The better marriage, children, house, etc. When we allow God's love to flow through us, we will be joyful when someone's life is blessed and filled with God's goodness. We will realize that as He blessed them, He can bless us. Our job is to abide in Him by being in His Word and applying it in our lives.

When a child feels loved and secure by their parent, they are not jealous of their siblings. When we feel secure in the love of Father God, we are not jealous of our Christian sisters when they receive their blessing before we receive ours. As we grow in intimacy and revelation of the love God has for us personally, we will not be jealous of others. Sibling rivalry stems from insecurity. However, if we understand His love for us personally and individually, there would be no room for rivalry, only LOVE. God's Love is infinite.

Webster's definition of **restrain** is to prevent someone from doing something; to keep under control.

Let's not allow ourselves to be restrained by anything BUT by LOVE. Let us be so compelled to love others, because of the Love we have been given.

God is calling us, His Body, His people, to link arms together and see beyond our differences, obtain one voice together, walking in power, love and grace. When are separated, we become weak and unable to build a wall of defense. But, when we are humble and link arms together, regardless of our theological differences, we can come together in unity. If you don't believe in miracles, or speaking in tongues, and another sister does, do not let satan divide His Body. Christianity is following Christ, who is our foundation. When we link arms together, like a moth to the flame, the world will recognize He is the way. They will be compelled by the Love they witness in those who call Him LORD.

As mothers, we can get so busy tending to the needs of our own families, we have very little left to give. There are strategies from God to reveal to you how you can apply balance in your life, so that you can help bring others to the revelation that they too are loved and sought after by God. I had a wonderful revelation as I was putting our youngest to bed one night. The Lord uses motherhood in my life to teach me many things. I believe it is because we as women, are anointed to bring forth life. Not just physically, but spiritually as well. We have the capability to bring forth life in people, to labor in prayer and love, so that those we pray for, can live the fullest life in Christ. We have the POWER to choose to speak words of encouragement, when everyone else is speaking negatively. As women, we have the POWER to nurture and nourish them with LOVE.

As I rocked my daughter, I received this revelation. A mother's milk increases or decreases depending on the needs of her baby. The milk increases, according to the demand of supply. When a mother has a healthy milk supply and has twins, her body will produce that which is needed. Just like a breastfeeding mother, as you increase in giving spiritually to others, God will give you the nourishment required so that you can continue to pour onto others. As you come to Him for yourself, He will give you all you need to expand His Kingdom.

When one becomes a parent in the faith to another, grace will increase so that the parent will have the nutrition for their offspring. God will see to it that His grace is sufficient for the task at hand. The more offspring, the more grace. The more you feed, the more He will give so that the supply will always be enough. Just the same, when a baby is sick, the baby nurses less. Therefore, when less milk is being consumed, less milk will be produced. If we give less to others, our supply is less. As you feed others, God will continue to feed you. What you give others is the overflow.

I do believe that we have to guard our hearts. You're not required by God to pour onto everybody, only those He leads you to. I believe it is the Holy Spirit's job to prompt us when we come to a situation that requires us to guard our hearts. If we do not like what we see around us, we have the ability to bring change by allowing the nutritional supply from the Holy Spirit to flow through us.

Can you imagine how misunderstood Jesus was all of His life? Can you imagine that people who were a witness to His life must have felt inferior, shameful, and didn't want Him too close to their sin? Can you imagine that all of His life, He was quite strange to everyone? What if Jesus allowed our sinful nature to keep Him from loving us? What if Jesus didn't see our potential—of what He could do through us by His love? If God loved the way we do, there wouldn't be a chance for our eternal life. Letting Him love through us takes courage. We must put our limitations aside and get over ourselves, so that He can raise up our lives with His supernatural LOVE. We are called to see the potential in others and labor to bring forth what we see in them through His full ascended vision.

We as women are bringers of life. Perhaps if we do not like what we see in those around us, our husbands, children, etc., we have not done our job to bring forth the labor that is required in the form of prayer and love. If you have, then keep on doing this. Every pregnancy has an expiration date. Eventually, the birth has to come!

If those you live with do not see Jesus in you, you are not serving where God has called you first. Those we live with, husband and/ or children, need to see us pouring into their lives first, and see the fruit of Jesus Christ in us. If they have not, it is because we have been so busy pouring into others, but neglecting the very field God has called us to. It is not effective, and it opens the door for satan to attack our homes. We cannot be Pharisees, hypocrites! Ask God to redeem the time that you have lost and to do a speedy work in your heart with the ability to witness His fullness to those you love the most.

Remember to say the prayer out loud so that you can hear what you are praying.

Father, help me represent you on earth. Help me abide in Your Spirit. Give me the opportunity to love and extend your mercy, I cannot do this without You. Help me knit people together, instead of watch division. Let me partner with You as You redeem the time, restore what has been stolen and allow crop failure on any seeds that I have planted that would oppose a healthy harvest. I recognize I am responsible for the condition around me, and I can choose to submit to You, which is life. I choose LIFE! I surrender to Your ways and I want to choose to represent Your Kingdom and side with Love, Grace, Mercy, and Your Presence. You give life to all that You touch. Help me do the same in Your name. Give me the grace to raise up people to know You, abide in You and trust in You, as I do the same. I give myself to You, for Your service. In Jesus name, Amen.

—Chapter 13—

Go Go Go Daughter of the King!

This study began when I started studying the life of Harriet Tubman. I had planned to use her life as the center of a teaching I did in 2012. A summary of Harriet Tubman's life is inspiring and triumphant. She was born a slave, who escaped slavery in the 1800's and helped lead approximately 300 people into freedom. She could have escaped and enjoyed it for herself, but she turned back to help those she loved and cared for. The love she held inside was stronger than fear, and her confidence came from the relationship she had already built with her God. Her life was built on perseverance, love for her brethren, and most of all her faith in God. She was known for her complete trust in God and following the leading of His voice. Among her people, she was known as "Moses" because she led the people out of slavery and into freedom. Since she was known to follow the voice of God, she would hear strategies from God as to how to rescue the slaves. God has the same strategies for you and myself.

Can we imagine how confident she had to be that it was actually God leading her? She had to be certain, otherwise she would be tortured or killed? Listening as to when to escape and where to hide? Can you imagine the witness she gave to God by recognizing the voice of God as she listened to find out where to hide, when to leave, when the guards were returning, where the children were, etc. Can you imagine how the slaves felt, that she would care enough to bring them along to freedom? Can you imagine the conversation she has had in Heaven with those she helped free? I can imagine many people thanking her for coming back, risking her life so that they could see faith in action, so they too could believe.

Can you imagine the conversation people will have about you—that you were covered in God's protection and you laid your life down by being a witness to His love as His daughter, and how you helped them to become free? I can imagine all of the people in Heaven thanking you for caring enough to invest the time it took to bring them love which brought transformation. Harriet Tubman lived a full life, no person took her life, she laid it down. Living a ripe life until she was near ninety years old, completing the mission God had given her.

As I was doing my study, I felt the Lord asking me, not to teach from her slavery, but from my own. Obviously, it would have been so much easier to stand before strangers and teach from another person's life. However, people don't want to hear how God's Word worked in someone else's life. People are looking for personal testimonies. People want to know how the Word can work in my life and in *your life*. I stand in awe of what the Lord chooses to do in everyday, ordinary people. Everywhere we go, there are slaves to something. Unless someone is living their life as Jesus directing them to, they are slaves and are not free. We cannot teach what we do not know. We cannot testify about something we do not witness. We cannot live on another person's understanding and revelation of God's Word. We have to experience Him for ourselves. Which means, we are going to have to do the work, but He will give us the grace to do it!

The reason why we got rid of the wounds in the beginning of this book, is because your body/spirit/soul can only contain so much. Once your vessel is full, no more can be put in. Imagine an empty glass. When we have the "yuck" (rejection, anger, shame, trauma, disappointment) inside of us, we have to remove those things so that we can add the good things (Love, Faith, Forgiveness, etc.). Otherwise, the good and bad things get blended together and the good things get contaminated. A little poison, messes up the entire outcome. After we remove the "yuck", we need to continue to fill ourselves continuously, because living in this world uses up the measure we are given. That is why using the acronym will help us.

We need to fill ourselves with **P-** *PRAYER*. Then be **O-***OBEDIENT* to God's **W-***WORD*. In order to be obedient to His Word, we need to nourish ourselves with His Word. We need to stay in His presence and focus on who He is, which is when we **W-***WORSHIP*. We have to get rid of our selfish character and stay strong, which is why we **E-***EXERCISE* SERVING and we need to look like Him as His daughters and **R-***REPRESENT* HIM. If we do, then not only will we know we are HIS, but so will the enemy and the world.

In the previous chapters, we have released our wounds and asked our Father God to take them and make something new. With every journey, it is important that we know where we are going, so that we do not end up in the wrong place. The acronym we used will help us stay on the right journey towards the heart of our God: Prayer, Obedience, Word, Worship, Exercise Servanthood, Representative of the Kingdom. It is imperative that you keep going!

I am extremely proud of each of you, for setting out to complete the goal of going through this study with me and you succeeded. My prayer for you is that you would become like a strong tree planted deeply into the soil (Word) and planted by the river of Life (Holy Spirit). In order for the strong "tree" within you to continue to take deep root and to grow into complete maturity, we have to continue to stay in the Word. We have to face the giants that cause negative reactions within us.

Ask God what do you already have in your hand that you can impart to others? When God reveals to you your talents and gifts, ask Him how He has called you to use them to bring Him glory. Partner with God so that you can leave a legacy for the benefit of giving to the LORD who has given you so much. There are so many people that have left this earth that weren't planning on it. My prayer is that we would not just live life but we would live life with passion. Living life with such passion that we look to the world like a flaming torch leading them home straight into the arms of God.

I saw an image online of a man holding a torch straight up in the air with his right hand headed straight into the darkness. I felt the Holy Spirit impress on me to tell you, "I want you to become the torch that leads those in the darkness towards My heart." I believe that our lives can look like a torch lit up because we have received His love. He transferred us from darkness into His Light. When we have rejection, anger, and disappointment within us, it is so easy to focus on ourselves and our pain. The moment we turn our eyes to look at ourselves and our needs is the moment satan causes us to begin to fall. When you give the Lord your hurts, allow Him to heal you and love the hurt out of you. When you do, you will become the torch because you will be so grateful that He pulled you out of such torment and pain.

All the broken pieces of our lives don't make sense at all when we see them bit by bit. It doesn't make sense that I was abused as a child, or raped as a young girl, and so on. Piece by piece, they aren't beautiful. As a matter of fact, some of them are downright ugly. BUT, when we give them to God, the Master Artist, He takes them. He glues them together with His Love, His Mercy, His Grace, His Forgiveness, and bit by bit, they become a mosaic piece of art... a Mosaic Art Piece that only He, the Great Artist can make. His masterpiece within you is being formed right now! When the Master Artist has received all of the pieces that You have submitted to Him, He can form a new one- of- a-kind art piece, a new you, His creation. You will become one who has been sanded, buffed and prepared for His purposes and able to bring more captives to freedom. Although God did not bring you the pain, He can use the pain for His glory for resurrecting what was once dead. He will allow all things to come together so that we can leave a legacy built on His unfailing love which brings transformation.

Always remember, God never hurt you, He never caused such evil and catastrophic occurrences in your life. God loves you so much that He doesn't want to allow you to stay where He picked you up. The resurrecting power of God can resurrect all that you need, not only for us to receive salvation, but the power that brings transformed and resurrected people on earth.

Will you show the world what a Daddy's girl you are by giving Him your life because He paid for it? Will you stop allowing people to abuse you, not recognizing your worth? Jesus says, *"Don't give pearls to swine"* (Matthew 7:6). Don't give yourself to someone that cannot receive you or value you or treasure you for the purpose you are intended. It is good to serve the Lord and it is fine to say "no" when a "pig" wants your "pearls". There are a lot of "pigs" who are not prepared to wear "pearls". You are too good to live like the daughters that belong to the world. They are blind, but you my sister, are not. You were meant for so much more and are chosen to be a torch in the darkness to lead others home. Your life was meant to be on display so that others would want to join His family of love, because He wants to reveal Himself to them, by touching your life with His goodness.

> *"The Spirit of the Lord is upon YOU, because He has anointed YOU to preach good news to the poor, He has sent YOU to proclaim freedom for the prisoners and recovery of sight for the blind, to release the oppressed, to proclaim the year of the Lord's favor."* ~ Luke 4:18 NIV (emphasis added)

When you grasp the true revelation of your True Daddy, you will realize you are to bring others into the family. You have received a new heritage, one that comes with no sickness, no lack, no depression, no type of poverty (emotionally, physically, or spiritually). You are to be a spiritual mother or sister to someone else and bring them along with you. I sense God searching the earth looking upon the masses of people and asking, "WHERE ARE YOU DAUGHTERS OF THE MOST HIGH? WHERE ARE YOU? RISE UP DAUGHTERS WHO BRING

DAUGHTERS. RISE UP DAUGHTERS! STAND FIRM IN ME! RISE UP KNOWING YOUR DADDY CALLS YOUR NAME!

I AM YOUR HEALER. I AM YOUR SOURCE. I AM YOUR PROVIDER. I AM YOUR FREEDOM. I AM YOUR ROCK. I AM THE ONE WHO CALLED YOU INTO EXISTENCE AND I AM THE ONLY ONE WHO'S OPINION OF YOU HOLDS TRUE VALUE! I AM WORTHY! I AM HOLY! I DELIGHT IN YOU! YOU BRING ME PLEASURE. LOVE IS ON MY MIND WHEN I THINK OF YOU."

> *"The Spirit of the Lord is upon YOU, because He has anointed YOU to preach good news to the poor, He has sent YOU to proclaim freedom for the prisoners and recovery of sight for the blind, to release the oppressed, to proclaim the year of the Lord's favor." ~* Luke 4:18

It is my hope and the hope of those that have pioneered the way for your faith, especially our God who hung on the cross, that you would take this baton and run the race. If you keep the Holy Spirit as your coach, you will run the race with endurance, He will guide you and reveal anything that is preventing your running ability. He will make sure when you do not have a cheering section, that you hear Him loud and clear and know that all of Heaven cheers for you. When you feel tired and weary, He will make sure you are refreshed. He that has begun the good work in you, IS FAITHFUL TO COMPLETE IT. ~ Philippians 1:6

Receiving the love of God in places that were concealed deep within our soul bring indescribable freedom that cannot be articulated, but can only be expressed through a transformed life. Remember, just like in the life of a butterfly, transformation takes place one process at a time. **GO, GO, GO, Daughter of the King**.... Take your position, for the Kingdom of God goes with you.

About the Author

Monica Ibarra is an ordained minister of the Gospel of Jesus Christ, who depends wholeheartedly on the Holy Spirit. Equipped with the Word of God and the close bond she shares with her Abba, Father, Monica candidly unveils her stories of past pain for the purpose of exposing the enemy's tactics to shine light where darkness is in operation. In 2011, Monica was led to birth *Monica Ibarra Ministries*. Through this ministry, many women's lives have been impacted in profound ways.

"Take Your Position Daughter" is based on Monica Ibarra's teaching series, "Take Your Position, Daughter of the KING." This God-inspired series has proven to be an effective tool that brings women healing from emotional pain and propels them toward a deeper intimacy with the LORD. She is passionate about equipping believers to know the LORD and reveal the Kingdom of God both in word and in action.

She and her husband co-labor for the work of the Kingdom and have been married for over 25 years and have three children. It is often that Monica and her husband have a full house with many children and young adults in order to disciple and train them in the LORD. Her life's motto is, "In everything, let the LORD be known".

Contact Information

Monica travels to preach wherever the Lord leads and helps women experience the redemptive power and freedom through the finished work of Jesus Christ. To connect with her or to invite her to speak at your event, visit:

Facebook "Monica Ibarra Ministries"

Website: www.monicaibarra.org

Email: mibarra316@yahoo.com

If by reading this book you were blessed in any way, please consider leaving a review to help me spread this message of hope and healing.

1. Go to www.amazon.com
2. Search for "Take Your Position Daughter by Monica Ibarra. 3. Scroll to the bottom and click on "Write a Customer Review" 4. Rate the book (out of 5 stars) and write your review.

Please note, you do not have to purchase the book from Amazon to write a review. However, you must have an amazon account. Thank you, in advance, for your positive review!

www.ingramcontent.com/pod-product-compliance
Lightning Source LLC
LaVergne TN
LVHW020058090426
835510LV00040B/2146